BEYOND MONEY

Beyond Money
Ex-IRS Agent Reveals How to Master U.S. Tax Codes to Build Wealth and Financial Freedom

Natasha J. Verela

©2024 All Rights Reserved. No portion of this book may be reproduced, stored in a retrieval system, or transmitted in any form or by any means- electronic, mechanical, photocopy, recording, scanning, or other-except for brief quotations in critical reviews or articles without the prior permission of the author.

Published by Game Changer Publishing

Paperback ISBN: 978-1-964811-77-2
Hardcover ISBN: 978-1-964811-12-3
Digital ISBN: 978-1-964811-13-0

www.GameChangerPublishing.com

Read This First

Just to say thanks for buying and reading my book, I would like to give you access to a special bonus training, no strings attached!

Beyond Money

Ex-IRS Agent Reveals How to Master U.S. Tax Codes to Build Wealth and Financial Freedom

Natasha J. Verela

www.GameChangerPublishing.com

Table of Contents

Introduction 1

Chapter 1 – My Story 5

Chapter 2 – Never Leave Ordinary Income on the Table 21

Chapter 3 – The Four Tax Codes You Need to Succeed 41

Chapter 4 – Business Structure 73

Chapter 5 – Business Ownership & Strategy 85

Chapter 6 – Real Estate Investment and Strategy 99

Chapter 7 – How to Maximize Your Tax Saving While Building Wealth 121

Chapter 8 – The Ideal Marriage 137

Conclusion 143

Introduction

When I was asked what this book is for, my immediate answer was *to help people build wealth through the United States Tax Code.* The truth is that I didn't even think of wealth. I thought of freedom. I just wanted *enough money* to live comfortably. For me, that meant not reporting to any office, not reporting to any superiors at work, not having to attend meetings, and not having to wake up at 5 a.m. to be at my desk by 8:30 a.m. I was a New Yorker, so our method of transportation was buses and trains. The average New Yorker doesn't live in Manhattan. We live in the outer boroughs or even the suburbs, where the commute is *easily* 1.5 hours on average.

I wanted to be free of all the exhaustion that came with being a worker bee. That meant money—lots of it. The only way was to operate like the wealthy, to learn to do as *they* do, whatever that is, because, to me, they were *free*.

So, who is this book for? Me, in the sense that I am *you*, the average American. Those who spent all their life hearing, "Go to school, get a job, buy a home, have a family." The average Generation X or Millennial who accumulated burdening student loans they will never get out of because jobs aren't paying enough. And with current living expenses, they will almost never get out from underneath those expenses. Those who were not taught financial literacy because their elders didn't know it.

The one sibling who has to help the family because they are the ones who *made something of themselves*, whatever that means. The average cubicle worker who hates waking up at 5 a.m. to be at work at 9 a.m. The average wage earner who went to college chose a major at 19 for their 30-year-old self and is now miserable. Those with billable hour jobs that push them to cry in the bathroom stall at work because they can't afford to quit and can't take the forced, above-and-beyond requirements of staying late as the norm. The person who's scared to start a business with their passion for "cheese sculpting" because they lack confidence but have exceptional skill. I am all of these people. Five jobs and 19 years later, I pulled myself out. It wasn't a fast road, but it was a sure road. The truth is, most of us don't aim for millions upon millions overnight. It would be nice, but the reality is most of us just want *freedom*. That looks different for everyone on a daily basis, but at the core, it's time and the ability to live comfortably without stress.

One person might like a mobile home and a simple life; another may want to live in a penthouse. Either way, it's different for everyone and usually requires freedom—you need to own your own time. Now that I have freedom, I understand why Warren Buffett lives in the same house he bought in 1958 and follows a down-to-earth lifestyle, even as the 10th richest man in the world in 2024.

What are you going to get from this book? *An understanding that the wealthy operate within the tax code first and foremost.* They don't rely on ordinary income (which is W-2 income), like most of us do. They are business starters and real estate investors who never rely on one source of income and never put their hopes in the *American Dream*, which is your W-2 plus your primary residence. I am the average Joe. I came from an immigrant father from Haiti and a wage-earning mother.

I was taught to go to school, get as much education as possible, and make a good salary—whatever that means. I want to share my personal story for inspiration, to show that the wealthy aren't just those in jets and high-end cars. Most of us are self-made, and success is achievable. It's not out of reach.

I want to show how the tax code works by distinguishing between two approaches. On the one hand, there's the traditional path, which involves getting multiple degrees, going into debt, and spending most of your working life paying it off for the sake of bragging rights. On the other hand, there's what wealthy people actually do: *They build successful businesses.* If you have an idea for a business, pursue it. If you don't invest in yourself, you'll continue to invest in Uncle Sam through your withholdings with no return.

Learn how to let go of money in the right way and how operating within the tax code can help you build wealth. Most of my education didn't come from college but from being in a room with wealthy people, examining their tax returns, balance sheets, and income statements, and engaging in conversations with them. Keeping your net earnings too tight will keep your withholdings in Uncle Sam's grip. Instead, focus on what's not being deposited in your bank account.

The reality is that the *American dream* isn't dead. It never was. It was packaged, sold, and bought by many of us and is fueling the actual dream of the wealthy. You buy your dream home for $400,000 at a 7.03% interest rate over 30 years. Your down payment is, say, 20%, which is $80,000 (all of your savings and most likely also coming from your retirement funds). Your monthly mortgage is around $2,100, not including property taxes. Do you know how much you actually paid for the home over 30 years? $768,750.92! Do you know who made that money? The investors/lenders! You just paid over $368,000 to investors to borrow $400,000 for your home. You were the consumer. The investors made the money. Now, think larger: There are millions of borrowers across the country. These same investors are making *billions* overall.

How are you paying your mortgage? By working your wage-earning job. Who's paying you? The company. Who makes the ultimate profit? The owner(s) of the company. So, you are receiving wages to pay your mortgage so that you can make money for your employer and, in turn, use that money to make money for investors. Everything you have been sold is for the benefit of the wealthy. You are working for their dream, packaged and sold to you as your dream.

I am writing this book so that you understand not only how to build wealth but also how to understand the flow of money to build wealth. To help you change your relationship with the dollar because the dollar is the lowest-yielding asset in the world. It depreciates over time due to inflation. You were told to *save, save, save!* While the wealthy are taught to *invest, invest, invest!* Saving depreciates the dollar. Investing appreciates the dollar. You saved for your home so investors can make money off of you. You work for your employer so they can make money in their company. You think like a saver. I want you to think like an investor.

This is not another book about money. I focus on very specific components of the tax code. I don't speak on digital currency or foreign exchange (FOREX). I don't tell you to buy stocks. I don't truly believe that is what will get the average person out of the ultimate bondage. I focus on one very specific aspect of wealth: the U.S. tax code. Why? Because that is the vein of wealth in the United States. To go even further, I focus on very few aspects, as you don't need to be a rocket scientist to get this rhythm.

The purpose of this book is to give you a way to start executing the necessary changes to grow your bottom line. *I'm living proof it can be done.*

CHAPTER 1

My Story

THE BEGINNING

I think it's important to tell my story, as it gives perspective. I was not born into money. I didn't have a trust fund. I come from an immigrant family on one side. My dad is from Haiti, and my mother was second-generation, born in the U.S. with Jamaican and American roots. I grew up in Queens, New York, and moved around... a lot. I did what many in my generation, Gen X, were advised to do: *Go to college.* The idea was that you could earn degrees, and the more degrees you had, the more money you could make, leading to a better life, right? So, I went to SUNY Albany in January 1998 and graduated in 2002 with a Bachelor of Science in Economics. Afterward, I worked for less than a year as an auditor at Trans World Entertainment, which owned FYE stores where people bought music CDs before streaming became prevalent.

In the fall of 2002, I returned to school at The College of St. Rose, also in Albany, New York, to pursue a Master of Science in Accounting. I graduated in 2004 and immediately found a job as an audit consultant in New York City. Getting a job back then wasn't too challenging, as recruiters played an active role in the hiring process. My master's degree also made it easier to secure interviews and even get hired on the spot.

2004

This is where my journey truly began. My first *adult* salary was $51,000 a year, but I had $85,000 in student loans. For a year, I worked for an international team at an oil field services company, performing field audits for governmental compliance in various locations worldwide. I traveled to Moscow and Siberia, Mumbai and New Delhi, the UAE, Norway, and many other places while stationed in Paris, France. Although this might sound glamorous, the reality was 10-12 hour workdays, leaving me feeling like a McDonald's employee in terms of hourly earnings. I was exhausted, and some days, I struggled to function due to lack of sleep.

2005

After about a year, I left and began working for a media and entertainment giant, allowing me to get a salary increase. I started as a senior auditor, earning $71,000 a year. This new role involved performing financial and operational audits, similar to my previous job, but this time with national rather than international travel. However, I didn't stay long, as my primary goal was to continue increasing my salary.

2006

I was hired at a prestigious law firm as a senior auditor/accountant. My starting salary was $98,000, with bonuses to come. By this time, I was in my late 20s and on my third job out of grad school. This time, I didn't have to travel anywhere. Again, I stayed for over a year and saved all my money, including any bonuses. I was a saver. That's what I was taught—*save, save, save!*

2008

I ended up leaving and started preparing taxes under my own company as a sole proprietor. I purchased professional filing software, got my PTIN, registered my fingerprints with the local police station, and fulfilled any other requirements.

Before I left the law firm, I applied to the IRS for the position of Revenue Agent in the Large and Mid-Sized Business Division (now called the Large Business & International Division). I was called for an interview in early May of 2008, and my first day was June 24, 2008. And so began my journey into the veins of real wealth in the United States: the Tax Code. I took a significant pay cut because public sector jobs don't pay as much as the private sector in general.

I still had a lot of student loans: $25,000 from my undergrad and $60,000 from my grad school, totaling about $85,000. I brought home about $1,300 every two weeks in my first job, but I just couldn't tackle my student loans. And so I kept going for a new job every year to get a bump up in salary, which is what most people do.

2010: THE CONDO

About three years into my employment at the IRS, I went into contract for my condo. Again, I thought, *Oh, this is the path: Go to school, get degrees, find a good job, work your way up, buy your first property, and so on.* I wasn't thinking about investment but rather about survival and hitting *adult* milestones. I closed on my condo in downtown Brooklyn, NY, on September 1, 2010. The 10% down payment, along with closing costs, wiped out all my savings, especially with student loan payments to manage. The combination of mortgage payments, Homeowner Association (HOA) fees (also known as "common charges"), and student loan payments ate into my paycheck. For reference, **HOA fees** or **common charges** are monthly fees for condominium owners that go toward maintaining the common areas of the building or community. While single-family homes and townhomes sometimes have these fees, condominiums *always* do.

Shortly after moving in, I felt a bittersweet sense of accomplishment: *I did it... all by myself. I have a luxury condo in one of the most desirable areas of NYC.* Then I realized there was no money in my account, and I needed my next paycheck. I felt nervous, having never experienced such vulnerability before. I was used to saving and having financial wiggle room. Before purchasing my condo, I had saved up a lot by living well below my means—renting rooms while my friends rented apartments and keeping my old car while they bought new ones with large payments. I was very frugal, and suddenly, I was back to square one. Now, I had a mortgage, HOA fees, student loans, and other living costs.

This vulnerability triggered anxiety. I realized I had to keep my job because my ability to pay my mortgage and HOA fees depended entirely on my income. This led me to see the matrix of the *American Dream*.

My HOA fees increased almost immediately because it was a new construction. At the time, I didn't know that developers or builders could artificially lower HOA fees to make units look more appealing to buyers. When purchasing a condo or any HOA community property, monthly fees are a key factor as they contribute to the overall cost outside the mortgage. If you default on HOA fees, the Homeowners Association can force the sale of your property, potentially causing you to lose your home. Thus, many potential buyers place heavy emphasis on these monthly charges, which cover the common areas and benefits like a doorman, porters, landscaping, elevator maintenance, and community water and sewage.

In my case, the condo developer/builder was subsidizing the building's monthly operations with his own funds and possibly with construction funds as well, which led to an inaccurate sense of operational costs and artificially low HOA fees.

It's important to note that in every HOA community, a board is typically formed soon after the units start selling. This board comprises owners from the community who oversee the interests of the units.

Once the developer/builder formed the board, all operations and finances became transparent. At this point, barely half of the units were sold and occupied, with about 30 out of 60 units remaining unsold. Simultaneously, we were notified that the developer/builder was in the early stages of defaulting on the construction loan due to slow sales. As a result, the building went into **receivership**, meaning a court-appointed person (a receiver) assumed custodial responsibility for the property, particularly as the developer could not meet its financial obligations.

The board took over the finances from the receiver but soon realized there wasn't enough money to cover all the bills: water and sewage, building electricity, doorman salaries, elevator maintenance, porters for daily cleaning, and even the shuttle to the train station. It was a mess!

We had about half the units empty, as they were unsold. During the developer's attempt to stay out of foreclosure, an investor stepped in and purchased the unsold units, ultimately at a bulk discount (ahh, capitalism). By now, I guess you're wondering why I need to tell this story. Keep reading.

Now, we had a condo building in which one person/entity owned about half the units and subsequently rented them out, as investors do. What does that mean for the owners? Financial bondage.

Let me explain why. Because of the events that occurred, the condominium building failed to meet the minimum financing standards of government-backed/conventional mortgages. Most homeowners have a government-backed mortgage through their lender. This simply means that if someone defaults on their mortgage to the lender, one of three federal agencies has insured the loan: The Federal Housing Administration (FHA), the U.S. Department of Agriculture (USDA), or the Department of Veterans Affairs (VA). This insurance protects the lender in the event you cannot pay your mortgage, usually referred to as **defaulting**.

A condominium building or community that doesn't meet conventional lending guidelines is termed **non-warrantable**. What specifically makes a condominium community non-warrantable?

1. The building ownership is concentrated, with a few owners.
2. The building units are mostly rental units.
3. The building lacks cash reserves (derived from HOA fees).
4. The building is in litigation.

As you can see, we checked all the boxes. This means that if any unit owner wanted to sell, they would only be able to sell to an all-cash buyer. Anyone who needed a mortgage to purchase a unit would be denied because of the non-warrantable status of the condominium building. See how this could be a problem? This is why I *do not* recommend condos as an investment strategy.

The Rise in HOA Fees

Tying this into my journey, after realizing that the current monthly HOA fees were not enough to cover the building's operations and maintenance, we (I was on the condominium board) had to do the inevitable—raise the monthly fees on the owners. You can imagine being the bearer of bad news. We aren't talking about $20 or $30 increases. It was significant.

Assessments

In addition to increased monthly HOA fees, we had assessments. These are one-off expenses that are usually substantial, requiring large amounts of funds to rectify immediately. Particularly with new development, you might have things that weren't engineered correctly, and now you have a one-time expense that has to get fixed, and that gets passed on to the owners. Assessments can last six months or years, depending on the issue. We had hot water issues due to incorrect engineering, building codes that were due, and incorrect materials used to build. You're thinking, *You didn't see this before you bought it?* No one does. You only see surface-level issues. Everything is new and shiny, so you assume "New = No problems." In my case, the building needed upwards of a million dollars to bring it up to code. In NYC, this can be very costly: engineers, lawyers, architects, contractors, etc. This extra expense was now assigned to each owner of the units in the building and lasted at least for the duration of my ownership.

So here I was, with the other owners, a significant increase in HOA fees and assessments on top of assessments. I was drowning financially. I was *stuck*. I couldn't sell because no lender would give a mortgage to a buyer—non-warrantable status, remember. My only option was to rent the unit out to relieve myself of the financial strain on my income. And so began my journey as an investor.

2013

Because, in purchasing my property, I had taken advantage of a $8,000 credit under President Obama's administration, I had to occupy the unit for three years. Three years of financial strain. In the third year, I contacted a broker to list my unit for sale. I thought maybe I'd get lucky and someone would offer cash, or maybe the banks changed their mind about the building (*I can hear the laughter in my head as I write*). Needless to say, I realized the building was doomed to its non-warrantable status. It was never going to change, as one of the main issues was that the investor owned about half the units, and they were all renters.

I ended up finding long-term renters at first. The market rate rent covered my monthly carrying costs, including the HOA and assessments. Now, I did this initially because I wasn't thinking about taxes; I was thinking about relieving my paycheck from such a financial burden, which is what most people think about—the money that hits their account.

It came time to file my tax return, which I had always prepared on my own. I saw that I actually got a significantly larger refund because now that I was renting my condo, I was able to take all kinds of expenses. I started to see how it affected my return just from the short amount of time that I rented it. Under the tax code, up to $25,000 may be deducted as a real estate loss per year as long as the individual's adjusted gross income is $100,000 or less. My salary was definitely under $100,000. We will talk more about strategy in the later chapters.

Having seen this newfound financial windfall via the tax code, I did more research. The irony is I knew the benefits of real estate; I just didn't internalize them. I was so hardwired to operate as a *saver* and not an *investor*. This is where the change took place in my thinking.

2014

In 2014, I went straight to a conventional lender and started the pre-approval process for purchasing another property. I was denied and told I had a high debt-to-income ratio. I had no credit card balances, just my condo mortgage, which was being paid by my tenants, and my student loans and living expenses. It turned out my student loans were the blockage in my financial arteries. I was still in a vulnerable position. I was about to turn 35 and was still relying on one source of income. I couldn't purchase more property. I couldn't put a dent in my student loans. My paycheck was not increasing. I felt like a trapped rat. Sound familiar?

I asked myself, *What can I do?* I looked at my retirement plan, which is known in government as a Thrift Savings Plan. I thought, *I can take this money out and pay off my student loans*, as they had become both an emotional and financial barrier. I felt trapped in a cycle: going to work, collecting rent, and hoping to eventually unload my condo (which depended on the market). I felt the need to free myself from this cycle and gain financial flexibility. I wanted room to breathe without worrying about each paycheck's allocation. I realized I needed to get rid of the boulder of student loans, or I would be *stuck* in a paycheck-to-paycheck cycle until retirement.

So, I took it upon myself and did some analysis. At my current interest rate and principal balance, I would end up paying off my student loans in 15 years. That meant 50 years old. I was 35. What could I do if I removed the student loans from my balance sheet? My credit would go up for sure. My debt-to-income ratio would be attractive. I could now contribute to my retirement plan at maximum because there would be no more student loan payments. So, I took a deep dive, pulled money out of my retirement account, and paid off my student loans in full. Now, I had little to no retirement funds and no student loans. I immediately began contributing to my retirement plan at maximum since I was relieved of student loans. My credit score shot up over 800 and the financial doors started to open. I know what you're thinking: *Didn't you have to pay taxes and penalties on that early distribution?* Yep, but because I had real estate, I was able to offset any of the taxes due, as mentioned previously. You can utilize up to $25,000 in losses if your adjusted gross income is under $100,000, which mine was. We will talk about other strategies later in this book so you understand the specifics.

I started to do more research on the tax advantages of owning property. I started to really pay attention to the tax returns I was examining, soaking all of it in. A tax return tells a story. I had direct access to the tax code as a revenue agent in the IRS and direct access to specialists. I also had my own experience, but now I was internalizing it *very* differently. I was unlearning and relearning.

I saw there were long-term and short-term rental rules and that I could effectively offset my W-2 income or any other active income by utilizing real estate. Shortly after, I changed my investment property to a short-term rental so that I could take advantage of short-term rental rules. Now, it was a condo, so there were HOA restrictions called bylaws. Luckily, I had room to utilize my condo as a short-term rental. I will discuss why I had to do short-term rentals instead of long-term rentals later in this book when we discuss business and real estate tax strategies.

I know what many of you are thinking again: *You touched your retirement and sacrificed compounding interest. You lost money!* The reality is I didn't lose anything. I didn't count on what could happen; I handled what was actually happening. I ran my own numbers, which I detail in my "Breaking Down Personal Credit" crash course, and the results were that I would have paid off my student loans at 50 years old or so if I had just kept going as is. More importantly, I could rebuild my retirement faster with maximum contributions instead of the minimum, as I needed the money for living expenses.

I wanted my freedom now. The younger you are, the more time you have to maneuver, the more flexibility. It just made sense. Once I released that chain of student debt off my legs, I decided now to look at how to unload my condo again. I put it back up for sale but still couldn't unload it. I had the same issues. The condo was still and forever non-warrantable. The boulder started to feel heavier and heavier. While I had a positive tax impact from being a landlord, I still had cash flow issues.

2016

Now, I still didn't have any investment knowledge, just tax, but it was trial and error, and I was really good with numbers. So, I purchased another property. It was a single-family home bought from **flippers**, people or entities that purchase homes, renovate them, and sell them for profit. I thought the property was a great investment because it was in a highly desirable area. I also noted that the property taxes were not that high. I still hadn't learned my lesson. I wanted to live on the property. I thought, *No HOA, all good.* Not quite.

2017

A year later, I got a bill for my property taxes because of the new sale. It turns out that when a property has a new sale recorded, the property taxes are reassessed. My taxes doubled. And I was like, *Crap, I knew this was too good to be true!* This was my second mistake. My condo was also my primary residence, but I thought buying a single-family home would remove a lot of the issues because I didn't have to worry about HOAs, I didn't have to worry about other unit owners affecting my ability to sell, and so on. I learned that the single-family home was not really the move for me. Again, this was trial and error. Nobody was teaching me, but I was learning.

I ended up selling the property a year later because, once again, costs outside of the mortgage increased, such as property taxes, which ate into my paycheck. Are you sensing a theme here? Because I had little equity, I had to learn how to sell the property myself, FSBO (For Sale By Owner), as I couldn't afford to pay broker fees and still break even. Remember, it had only been a year. I did my research and placed the property on an online MLS listing broker. I paid a nominal fee of around $400 or so. I held open houses and had an FSBO sign in the front yard. My property was in pristine condition, as it was newly renovated from the purchase.

I held about three open houses before I got an interested couple who wanted to move into the neighborhood because their family lived there, and they had no broker. We ended up closing the deal successfully, and I made a small profit. Now, I was seeing the impact of real estate not only through taxes but through sales. I had to figure out what to do next. What was my next move? That doggone condo was still there. My paycheck was still the same. I had no student loans so I could move financially with more flexibility.

2019

By now, you're thinking this book is all about real estate. Nope. I am just letting you in on my journey, and this is how it unfolded. In late 2019, I learned about a program on how to become financially free through investing in multifamily investment properties. I became a student, went to an in-person seminar, and met the person who teaches, and they became kind of a mentor. We began speaking about our backgrounds. They mentioned how I was very knowledgeable in taxes and that maybe I should teach everything I knew, given my background, especially as an examiner. It dawned on me that I could teach. I'd been working for the IRS for a while, and I'd had co-workers come up to me and ask me, "Have you ever thought about teaching because you teach really well?" Because there were a lot of complex topics in tax that many people didn't know about. Even as an IRS Agent, you don't know the whole tax code. I did a PowerPoint presentation at work and passed it around to my colleagues. I received really good feedback, so I knew I had it in me.

So began my journey of educating on the tax code. But in the meantime, I still needed to purchase a multifamily. I bombed with the condo and semi-bombed with the single family, but I still made some money. And I learned how to sell on my own. If you can use a broker to do all the hard work, that's great. I didn't have the leeway because I had just bought my property a year before.

2020

During the pandemic, I started to build out "Tax Strategies Mastermind," a course that would teach about each type of business structure, how to form your structure, define your business activities, show you how to lower your tax liability with business ownership, and the tax advantages of real estate along with retirement planning. Simultaneously, I created my social media handle, "TheMoneynista," on Instagram and Facebook to grow awareness. Because I was still technically employed by the IRS, I couldn't give out any information that wasn't publicly available, and I couldn't teach or advise, especially for money, as it was a conflict of interest. I used this time wisely and strategically to build out my course modules and grow awareness on social media while still focused on purchasing a multifamily.

While putting my feelers out for a multifamily, I put more energy into building my social media following, so I started to curate my social media feed by pumping any extra money from my paycheck and savings into boosting my posts and growing my followers because we're in a time now when social media brings everybody together. Brick and mortar are not the standard anymore. You don't have to hand out flyers. I was still saving for my multifamily with each paycheck as well. In short, I made sure that all my wages from my employer went into real estate or building my business. By the end of 2020, I bought my first multifamily. I lived in one unit and rented out the other unit. By utilizing the tax code, I was able to offset all of my W-2 income. By early 2021, I left the IRS and became a full-time business owner and real estate investor. *This is the optimal combination for wealth building.*

2021 and Beyond

At the time I released the "Tax Strategies Mastermind" course in 2021, I did a pre-sale to make sure that I would have the interest and to see what the value of the course was. This was crucial. Most people can keep their jobs while pursuing their business interests. I could not. It was a conflict of interest, so I had to tread lightly. I had to not be an employee of the IRS if I was going to be educating others on the tax code as a business owner. By this time, I had curated my social media feed to a large following and had grown my email list. I had a good amount of pre-sales as people saw the value in my information, so I knew then I had to hand in my computer before releasing the actual content in the course.

My goal was to ultimately create an easy way to teach the average person how to grow their bottom line without confusing them. Anyone can give content, but teaching people to apply and execute is what will actually translate to wealth. This is not a spectator sport. This required active participation. The tax return gives anxiety to many people! So, I opted to teach with over-the-counter software: TurboTax. What's better than *not* putting pen to paper?! Let the software do the work. I wanted people to see their numbers in *real time* and understand how and when to apply the strategies I taught. I wanted them to have answers to questions like:

- What would happen if I spent more money on advertising?
- Do I have the money to expand?
- Do I have a tax liability now? If so, can I divert that money into my business to lower my tax liability?

- What would happen if I transitioned to a real estate investor?

How many of you would opt to pump money into your business interests or real estate rather than paying Uncle Sam through withholdings? I gave you my backstory so you understand how big of an impact shifting my ordinary income (wages from my employer) to business ownership and real estate has had on my net worth. My trial-and-error period was one thing, but my execution era was the defining factor in my overall financial freedom. I have been able to legally offset all of my tax liability by moving within the tax code and removing my housing costs. This is only done through business ownership and real estate.

In 2021, I purchased my second multifamily in Connecticut and did a complete rehab. The property was old but had potential. After all, I took a course from my mentor on how to analyze deals on multifamily rentals so I could choose my properties wisely and increase cash flow, and I had the tax knowledge to benefit from tax savings. Because of my renovation activities, I was able to benefit once again on my tax returns and offset all my tax liability. Again, I will talk about this in more detail later in the book with real estate strategy. I bought four more properties in 2022 and again offset all of my tax liability. At this point, I didn't have a housing cost due to the cash flow from the rentals and I was building wealth with the tax savings from all other income. And so I realized I had a winning formula for success. And then, in 2023, I finally bought my primary residence. All my rentals were fully occupied. I had enough cash flow to pay for my living costs. The cash flow was great, but the **tax flow** was amazing. Tax flow is a term I coined to define the amount of savings from offsetting your tax liability.

I eventually was able to unload my condo in 2022. It was my final attempt. I had an all-cash buyer, which circumvented the need for a conventional mortgage. I used the proceeds from that sale to purchase two of the four properties in 2022, which allowed me to utilize the real estate benefits to offset all of my tax liability. Again, I had the formula, so I decided to teach it in a visual way and not just pump out tax codes because teaching content really does nothing. I can teach the tax codes, but until you really see it and how it hits your return, it's not really valuable. So, I know the way I learned, which was visual, would benefit others. I knew the tax code, but I used what I had available to me to actually see the impact—the over-the-counter software TurboTax. With every move I made, I would plug it into the TurboTax file and let the software do the work. I would see which transactions would make those numbers in the little box go up and down. I knew this was effective. I knew this was a way to circumvent confusion and anxiety for those who really want to build wealth but are afraid of the complexities of tax. Visual was the key! It's one thing to know you can take a deduction; it's another to physically see how it actually impacts your true numbers.

I've helped students legally save millions of dollars in tax savings and reinvest that money into their children, properties, and their businesses. I wanted to teach people how important it was to move within the tax code because between leaving the IRS in 2021 and, to date, 2024, *I have quadrupled my net worth.* And so that's how important it is to move within a tax code. Once you move within a tax code, wealth will chase you because now you start to understand how money works, and you begin to understand the cycle of money and when to spend the money. I also learned not to hold so tight onto a dollar and how unimportant the dollar is when you go from that W-2 mindset to the business mindset. When you go to a mentality of building wealth, you start to think about the dollar in a very non-emotional way. You stop idolizing and hoarding it, and you understand the mindset of the wealthy and why they are so successful, even in times of economic downturn.

That's why it's important for me to teach visually, not just with content. You can see social media posts and talk to tax preparers, but you won't internalize it until you see it in your own numbers. I don't just focus on concepts but also on execution. Many business owners, real estate investors, freelancers, and even W-2 earners struggle financially because they don't track their numbers in real time, often delegating this task to someone else. This is a big mistake. Even if you have a tax preparer, they can't handle transactions for you, document activities to your benefit, or doctor up receipts. You have to do the work.

One of the main issues I face in my journey to educate is that many people adopt a "do-it-for-me" attitude. But this isn't feasible. Many people miss out on enormous tax savings because there's no magic switch a tax preparer can flip to save all your money. You must engage and prove with documentation. As I explain in more detail later, you must take responsibility or risk losing out. As the saying goes, "Give a man a fish, he will eat for a day; teach a man to fish, and he'll eat for a lifetime." I want you to have the knowledge to apply for a lifetime.

You must be involved. Some of the wealthiest people know their numbers in real time, not waiting for the end of the tax year to negate their tax liability. We know that legally reducing tax liability boosts your bottom line. We'll talk about how to get started in the next chapter. I'll often refer to my own story as an example to make it relatable and help you apply it to your situation. As I said in the introduction, I am *you*—not a trust fund baby or the child of wealthy parents. I am an average person who became above average by going against the grain.

CHAPTER 2

Never Leave Ordinary Income on the Table

Ordinary income is simply the wages you receive from your employer. Employer wages are taxed at some of the highest rates, and there's no real relief on the individual tax return. All in all, the following are allowable on your average Form 1040 (individual tax return):
- Itemized deductions
- Mortgage interest (primary residence)
- Property taxes (primary residence)
- Medical expenses that exceed 7.5% of your adjusted gross income
- Dependents and associated credits

None of these items move the needles of wealth and never will. This is not a strategy.

Does this mean you should quit your job? Of course not. There's no way we can just quit. I don't care what anyone says; you should never take a *leap of faith* without a plan. I kept my job until my plan was in execution mode. I *used* my ordinary income (wages) to engage in what I call extraordinary income. This is income that is favored by the tax code. In this case, and in most cases, it's business ownership and real estate.

This is where you start to understand money and how it works. It's a game of chess, not checkers. If you have money but don't understand it, you're going to lose it. Using the tax code, you can quadruple your net worth.

So, what do we do with our wages? Shift. This means moving your earnings into activities that shelter your tax liability. I'm not suggesting quitting your job today; you need that income. You can keep your job, but you must know how to show Uncle Sam that your W-2 income is not taxable. In Chapter 1, I discussed how I offset my ordinary income with business and real estate activities. While I had to leave the IRS due to a conflict of interest, you may not face that issue. You might be able to keep your W-2 job, and if you love it, great. However, you must use that income in a way that makes it non-taxable on your tax return.

If you know $1,500 will hit your bank account every two weeks, that's often what you focus on. But I want to break the chains and conditioning by shifting your focus to your withholdings—what doesn't hit your bank account because that's your money, too. You need to tell Uncle Sam, "Hey, this is my money, and I want it back."

So, what's your next step? Decide if you'll invest in rental properties or start a business. Many of you already have a business, are in the early stages, or are still hesitant. Procrastination is costing you money. I get the question often: "I'm a W-2 earner with a single-family residence and kids; what can I do?" The answer is always the same: *Business ownership and/or real estate investing.* That's it. Below is a depiction of the tax code hierarchy.

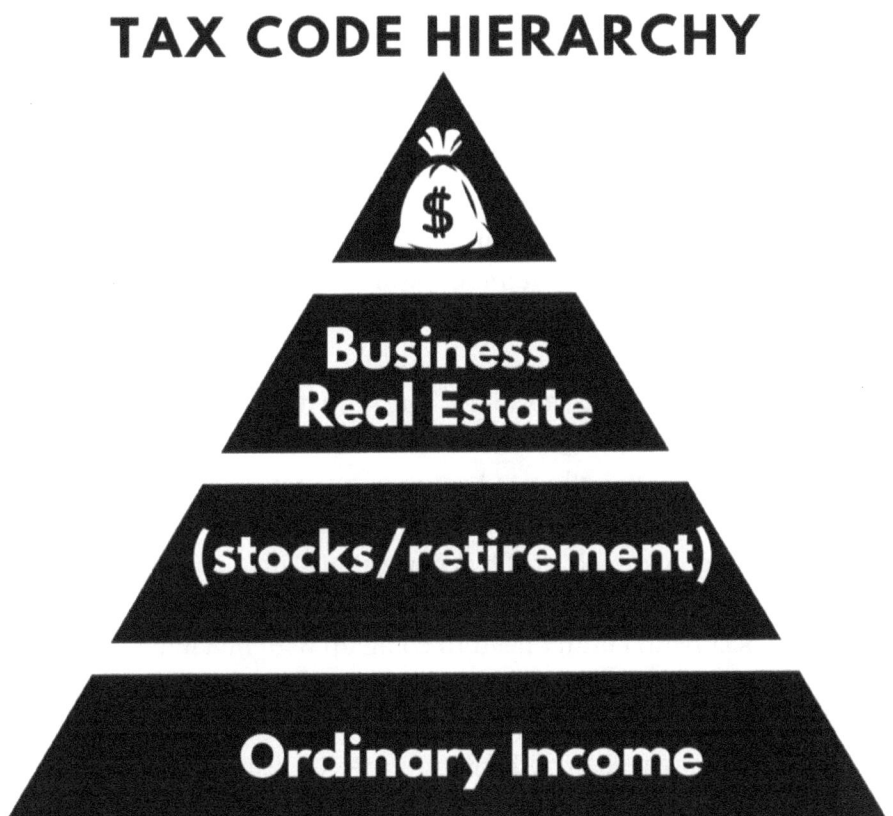

Many of you have a great business idea. Some of you are already in business, but you're not dedicated to it because you don't see immediate returns. Let me tell you, you won't get anywhere with that mindset. The global population is about 8 billion, with 340 million in the United States alone. Someone out there is your customer, client, or student. You need to use your human capital, speak to your audience, and let your tribe find you.

I'll use myself as an example. I had a W-2 job, but I translated my skill set into a business. It took me a little over a year, and although many don't want to invest that kind of time, the investment in yourself will multiply if you're dedicated.

On my mentor's advice, I dove into business ownership in 2020. While building my course, which took considerable time, I started with what was free—*social media*. I launched my Instagram page, "The Moneynista," on January 1, 2020, and began posting valuable information. I knew it would take time since I wasn't familiar with social media's capabilities and functionality. To boost my Instagram page's awareness, I pumped money into promoting my posts, using funds set aside from my paycheck. I cut unnecessary expenses like DoorDash, Uber Eats, and multiple streaming services. Posting was free, but building awareness was not.

By the end of 2020, my page had grown exponentially, thanks to boosting posts. I made my content valuable and relatable because, after all, I am most of you. I allocated some of my paycheck towards savings and some towards my business. In the midst of this, I also rebuilt my savings. I had a small profit from selling my single-family home (discussed in Chapter 1), and with a 5% down product from my lender as an owner-occupant, I didn't need to come up with much money. In total, it was $37,000. I remained frugal, saving every bit I could, and I also had a HELOC (Home Equity Line of Credit) from my condo.

By 2020, I engaged in both favorable tax transactions—business and real estate, as you may remember from Chapter 1. I was still a W-2 employee. Even though I hadn't officially released my product, "Tax Strategies Mastermind," and I was not officially structured under an LLC, I was still incurring start-up costs that would soon be tax-deductible. This included costs for the boosted posts, the platform for my course I was building out, the web hosting space, and the domain name www.themoneynista.com. I made sure to keep all expenses separate on a credit card and was careful not to intermingle personal expenses. Every year, I update the course on tax law changes and based on the feedback of my students. If they don't understand something, I go back, and I decide I'm going to redo the module so that they understand it. I'm constantly adding to it and people see value in it.

This book is intended to give you a great deal of information about operating in the tax code. It comprises two aspects: business ownership (non-real estate) and real estate investment, which is also considered a business activity, just a different tax code and set of rules.

BUSINESS OWNERSHIP

What are your next steps as a business owner? Holding onto that idea? *Get started.*

Your social media handles. Your domain name. Your web hosting service. These are all nominal costs. You don't have to have it done overnight. But you *do* have to start and finish. Start small and build out, but make sure you actually provide value. Be passionate. Love what you do. This is clichéd, right? Because it's true. Business owners often start with the idea of just selling and receiving income. They don't think of providing actual value. Will everyone love your offerings? No. That's okay. It's called the market. You won't please everyone. If you try to, you will fail. The goal is to provide an optimal result to your end user, also called your customer or, in my case, my students. What name do you have in mind for your business? Is the social media handle available? Grab it! Is your domain name available? You can search GoDaddy.com and see if it is. If so, grab it! Secure a web hosting service. I started with Squarespace as it was simple for newbies. I eventually graduated to Wix. Don't want to do the website? Hire someone. Fiverr.com is a great resource for web designers. You can easily purchase the domain name and web hosting service yourself and then outsource the design, including the logo. It doesn't have to be perfect. It has to be functional for your audience. Besides, as you grow, you can rebrand as needed. Again, these are nominal costs and activities.

Do you know what else is free? *Writing an ebook.* Are you an expert in your field? Provide literature that's valuable for a small fee or free. Free items are great for building your email list. You will need an email list provider. You can outsource this function as well once you sign up for a plan. I will provide you with a list of resources throughout this book that I used so you don't have to toil with research. Offer your valuable information in an ebook in exchange for an email sign-up. These are small-scale items that have a big impact. Keep all these costs on a separate credit card, clear of any personal expenses. We will get into personal versus business in the next chapter. *You are now shifting your ordinary income into extraordinary income.*

You can see the importance in the actual structure of the personal tax return (Form 1040) and the business tax returns, which include Schedule C on Form 1040, Form 1065 for multi-member LLCs and partnerships, Form 1120S for S corporations, and Form 1120 for C corporations.

Let's take a look at the structure of each and how it impacts your bottom line in the following diagram.

[Form 1040, U.S. Individual Income Tax Return, 2011]

As you can see from the image, the personal tax return has very little room for tax breaks. It may seem like it does, but as a tax professional, you don't get any benefits unless you are a sole proprietor, which provides for business deductions (see the image below).

Schedule C (Form 1040), Profit or Loss From Business (Sole Proprietorship), 2023. Department of the Treasury, Internal Revenue Service. Attachment Sequence No. 09. OMB No. 1545-0074.

Part I — Income
1. Gross receipts or sales. See instructions for line 1 and check the box if this income was reported to you on Form W-2 and the "Statutory employee" box on that form was checked
2. Returns and allowances
3. Subtract line 2 from line 1
4. Cost of goods sold (from line 42)
5. Gross profit. Subtract line 4 from line 3
6. Other income, including federal and state gasoline or fuel tax credit or refund (see instructions)
7. Gross income. Add lines 5 and 6

Part II — Expenses. Enter expenses for business use of your home **only** on line 30.
8. Advertising
9. Car and truck expenses (see instructions)
10. Commissions and fees
11. Contract labor (see instructions)
12. Depletion
13. Depreciation and section 179 expense deduction (not included in Part III) (see instructions)
14. Employee benefit programs (other than on line 19)
15. Insurance (other than health)
16. Interest (see instructions):
    a. Mortgage (paid to banks, etc.)
    b. Other
17. Legal and professional services
18. Office expense (see instructions)
19. Pension and profit-sharing plans
20. Rent or lease (see instructions):
    a. Vehicles, machinery, and equipment
    b. Other business property
21. Repairs and maintenance
22. Supplies (not included in Part III)
23. Taxes and licenses
24. Travel and meals:
    a. Travel
    b. Deductible meals (see instructions)
25. Utilities
26. Wages (less employment credits)
27. a. Other expenses (from line 48)
    b. Energy efficient commercial bldgs deduction (attach Form 7205)
28. Total expenses before expenses for business use of home. Add lines 8 through 27b
29. Tentative profit or (loss). Subtract line 28 from line 7
30. Expenses for business use of your home. Do not report these expenses elsewhere. Attach Form 8829 unless using the simplified method. See instructions.
31. Net profit or (loss). Subtract line 30 from line 29.
32. If you have a loss, check the box that describes your investment in this activity. See instructions.

As a business—and yes, a sole proprietor is still a business—you see that you have a plethora of opportunities to deduct expenses that lower your tax liability. Some of those expenses are also located on the first image of Form 1040, like your self-employed deductions (lines 28 and 29). If you are not engaged in business, these don't apply to you.

The same applies to other business tax returns. We will go through those structures in detail in Chapter 4.

The goal is to get you to understand that there's no tax relief outside of business activities, and that includes real estate. Don't believe me? The IRS publishes the *Internal Revenue Service Data Book*, which documents the gross collections by type of tax for the latest 10-year period every year. And every year, it looks the same, with the gap widening between taxes paid by individuals and taxes paid by businesses. See below:

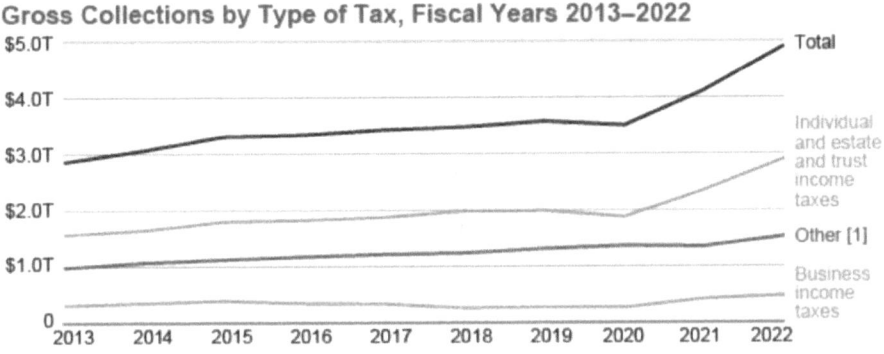

As you can see, businesses contribute the lowest amount of taxes. The most is collected from individuals. Breaking down the data into numbers, also available on the IRS website, $19.7 trillion is collected from individuals, estates, and trusts, while $3.4 trillion is collected from businesses. That's a $16 trillion difference over the last ten years, from 2013–2022. The numbers speak for themselves. *Which group do you want to be a part of?*

Do you think this data is only for large entities? Think again. According to the U.S. Chamber of Commerce, 99.9% of businesses in the U.S. are considered small businesses. There are about 33 million small businesses in the U.S. The big bad wolf of taxes isn't the large corporations. Small businesses benefit largely. The tax return doesn't care if your income is $100,000 or $10,000,000. You have access to the same tax benefits.

Operating in the tax code isn't a get-rich-quick scheme, but it is definitely a route to getting rich. We are going to look at the tax code for business owners and actual deductions and strategies later in this book.

REAL ESTATE

Almost everyone on the planet who is wealthy has their hand in real estate somehow. You don't have to love real estate, but you do have to be involved in some aspect to build wealth, especially in the U.S. What do I mean by **investor?** I mean **landlord**—purchasing property and renting it to a third party (tenant) and receiving monies in the form of rent per month (usually). Being a landlord is *extremely* beneficial in terms of the tax code. This is why the greatest wealth built by many almost always includes real estate. Let's look at the difference between your primary residence and a rental property.

Once again, I will use myself as an example. Remember my condo? I converted it to a rental due to my inability to sell. I immediately became an investor as the property was no longer my residence but a rental. Unlike me, you don't have to be backed into a corner financially to learn the benefits of being a landlord. You can be knowledgeable beforehand. I was a trial-and-error baby, and I learned due to circumstances that forced me to execute. You have the advantage of learning beforehand.

If you're living in your primary residence, what is your current tax benefit? If you have a mortgage, you can deduct your mortgage interest, which is on your Schedule A (Itemized Deductions) on your individual tax return. You can also deduct up to $440,000 in property taxes, also on your Schedule A.

Before 2017, when the Tax Cuts & Jobs Act (TCJA) was enacted, you would be able to deduct all your property taxes. There was a maximum placed on that amount because of this change.

What did the TCJA also do? It raised the **standard deduction**. The standard deduction is a specific dollar amount that reduces the amount of taxable income. This is called standard because all U.S. citizens who file a tax return are eligible. The amount is based on your filing status. For this explanation, we will focus on the four main filing statuses. Each year, there is an amount associated with each status for the standard deduction. For example, in 2024, the standard deduction for each status is as follows:

1. **Single:** $14,600
2. **Married filing jointly:** $29,200
3. **Married filing separately:** $14,600
4. **Head of Household:** $21,900

Why is this important? Ever since the TCJA went into effect, the benefits of being a primary resident homeowner have significantly declined.

Example: If you are single, your standard deduction for 2024 is $14,600. In order for you to qualify for more than that amount, your itemized deductions would have to be greater. So if you own a home, and your mortgage interest and property taxes are not greater than your standard deduction of $14,600 in our example, you will just get the standard deduction, like a renter. Same if you were married and filing jointly. If your standard deduction is $29,200, your mortgage interest and property tax deduction would have to exceed that amount to benefit. As we homeowners know, each year your interest amounts decrease as you start to pay more into your principal. Therefore, the amount to deduct decreases every year. Conversely, the standard deduction increases every year. This means that, soon enough, most homeowners will only be eligible for the standard deduction. There's no benefit on the tax return for your mortgage and property taxes.

Many will argue, "Well, I have equity, at least, and appreciation." These things are interconnected. The more appreciation there is for the value of your home, the more equity you have. This is a combination of you paying down your mortgage principal and the market commanding a higher price for your home.

Want to know a secret? Appreciation means nothing. It is a phantom. The market may command a price for your home; however, you do not have the funds in your account until you actually sell. Depending on appreciation is a dangerous game when it comes to wealth building. You must depend on constant cash flow.

"Flexibility" is key in the tax code when building wealth. I know many people can't just up and move due to family commitments, love for their school district, and not wanting to uproot their children. You must be able to maneuver, and this often feels uncomfortable. Sometimes, it seems like a setback when it's actually a setup for a comeback.

For instance, I gave up my luxury condo, which felt like a failure since I couldn't fully realize its value as a homeowner. I had envisioned it as my home, but we tend to develop emotional attachments that can harm our financial well-being. Emotional attachment can reflect our financial position, and many accumulate debt due to conditioning and emotions.

I encourage you to examine your situation. Housing is a huge expense, potentially second only to your tax liability. In some cases, it can even be larger. Then there are other living expenses, including childcare, which can be substantial. This is why it's crucial to recondition your financial mindset. We need to unlearn what we've learned.

I teach my students to do an exercise that I'd like you to try. Pretend you're converting your primary residence into a rental. This visualization exercise is effective if you're familiar with any over-the-counter tax software. Software like TurboTax and similar programs are underrated tools that are available at our fingertips. What would you save in taxes?

First, look up the current market rent for your property using free resources like Zillow.com, Redfin, or Realtor.com. Find comparable homes for rent that are currently listed. If you have a 4-bedroom, 3-bathroom home with a finished basement, look for similar homes to see their rental prices.

Next, use over-the-counter software like TurboTax Home & Business (I recommend the desktop version, not the online version). This is what we use in "Tax Strategies Mastermind." Instead of entering your home as a primary residence on your Schedule A, input it as a rental using the research you did online.

For example, if it's February, pretend you have rent coming in from March 1 to December 31. Say you found similar homes in your market that rent for $2,500/mo. In this exercise, you input rent collected for March through December for a total of $25,000 for the year you would report in rental income. Now, take the last Form 1098 that you received and plug in those numbers under the appropriate boxes labeled for mortgage interest and property taxes. The software will also calculate things like depreciation for you, which is an expense you automatically get as an investor. We will do a deep dive into this later and use this example for continuity purposes. Couple that with your regular input, like your W-2 income, your child dependents, and any other income, like interest from your bank, and look at the numbers that pop up on the screen to see the results. This is how I teach my students. You must see it visually to internalize it. We keep our tax files current during the year with input for any and all transactions, so we know our tax liability in real time without having to put pen to paper. Let the software do the work. We will go further into real estate in Chapter 7 with actual strategies because it gets better.

If you can't afford to buy a rental, why don't you take a look at the property you do have? You can do research to see if you can convert your primary residence into a multifamily. Check your zoning laws. Talk to contractors in your area who specialize in the conversion of single-family homes to legal multifamilies. Whether it's seeing if you can make it a multifamily or converting your single-family into a rental, the benefits are huge. I know what you are thinking: *Well, where am I going to live?* The tax that you save from converting your property to a rental and any potential cash flow could actually pay for wherever you're living, if that makes sense. *Investments should always come before your primary residence.* A lot of people don't see that, including me during my "trial-and-error" period, because they look for immediate problems. The goal is to look for immediate solutions. The amount of taxes that I've saved over the years completely paid for my living costs. It all started with the events that forced me to rent out my first property, which was intended for primary residency.

The next step in the exercise is to compare the results of your pretend rental to if you kept your home as a primary residence and just took the itemized deductions of your mortgage interest and property taxes. What is the difference in numbers? Significantly different. It gets *sooo* much better when we get into actual detail with strategy.

Another option is to research the market value of your current home if you own it and see if you can sell it and purchase a multifamily. Remember my first multifamily? I lived in one unit and rented the others. The lending guidelines are also more favorable to investment properties because lenders consider rental income. So don't think you won't be approved just because it may cost more. I was making six figures by the time I purchased my first multifamily, and I was approved for $740,000 on my own! *And* I still had the condo. I was able to get a 5% down-payment program, so I know many of you can too! And if you are one of those people who don't want to live next to someone else, the truth is building wealth requires flexibility. I now have my single-family home that I don't share with any tenants. Just four years after my first purchase, I was able to afford my own space. Again, small sacrifices and flexibility.

To be completely honest, it's not really a sacrifice. It's just unfamiliar, or you might have heard horror stories. Here's some news: Good tenants rarely get praise, but bad tenants are quickly aired out on all mediums. I've never had bad tenants to dissuade me from being a landlord. There are measures to protect landlords, which we'll detail later. Keep reading!

Many people who are considering starting a business may hesitate out of fear. But you can't be successful without failure. You need to see business differently. People think, *Well, you could fail.* It's a vulnerability. Your job could fire you. If my job had fired me—my only income source that paid for my property—I would've been in trouble. So either way, you're relying on something that's not secure. In 2008, many were laid off and couldn't pay their mortgages, relying on their employer as their sole income source. One economic disruption can leave you in a bind.

During downturns, the wealthy get wealthier because they don't rely on vulnerable sources. They have backups and are flexible enough to pivot. During the pandemic, I started my business and succeeded by providing tangible value. For the price of the Mastermind course, my students tripled, quadrupled, or more in tax savings. I didn't suffer; I even quit my W-2 job. I also had my multifamily property and purchased more. I've never had a rental vacancy for over a month, even though my properties aren't in "big cities" near Starbucks, fancy restaurants, or shopping areas.

The reality is that single-family homeowners with one income source, their jobs, often become renters during economic upsets. They can't afford another home, may go underwater on their current one, go into foreclosure, and become renters. It may sound harsh, but that's life. Before I was a homeowner, I was a renter. Even as an investment property owner, I was still a renter. I didn't purchase another primary residence until my investment properties could pay off their mortgages. I wish someone had taught me this earlier.

Five jobs and 19 years later, I finally understood the formula. Never rely on ordinary income and never leave it on the table. Allocate your paycheck to funding your freedom activities. Save for that down payment for an investment property. Start your own business. This is how wealth is secured. On average, 60% of Americans live paycheck to paycheck. That's not including those who are two or three paychecks away from financial ruin. I'd guess the percentage is a lot higher.

After really absorbing the information of the returns I examined, I knew how businesses secured their wealth and circulated money. Ninety percent of what I do during the year is favorable to the tax code. If it isn't favorable, I do not put effort into it.

Let's say you are a six-figure earner, around $100,000, and single. You don't own any investment properties, and you don't have any business activities, including freelancing. Your federal tax liability may be around $19,000 for the year. (I know because that was my liability as a single person with no kids.) If you use the withholding amounts throughout the year to engage in, say, starting your business, you can actually earn that money back into your account. In other words, you have the money; it's just that Uncle Sam is taking it. It's already out of your hands. So you have to engage in activities that tell Uncle Sam, "I actually am due that money back," or "I don't owe that money."

One of the important exercises I encourage for my students is to keep that tax planning file in over-the-counter software. We use TurboTax, for instance. Every month, we keep the file current with the latest paycheck year-to-date information (YTD) listed on the pay stub. Then, I ask them to plug in any business income and expenses or real estate income and expenses to date. They can tell what their current tax liability is—that little box that shows the refund or amount due. We love that box because it's visual as a result of a simple input. No surgery needed.

If a student has their current file, say in June, all of their information from January 1 to May 31 is in that file. They are able to tell if they have a tax liability. This gives them a chance to act in real time to offset that liability. For example, if I owe $15,000 because I had more income in a certain month, I have the option as a business owner or real estate investor to use the power of expenses to reduce that liability. I could increase the advertising costs in my business. If I needed a new computer, I could purchase one and expense it. If I had a property that needed a new bathroom vanity because the old one was falling apart, I could have that purchased and installed and deduct it. Perhaps I've been putting off getting a new hot water heater for a property. Now's the time to get one so I can expense it and offset my current tax liability. All of these things can be considered **expense acceleration**—meaning we may not otherwise engage in these expenses if we didn't have a huge tax liability. They are legitimate and legal to deduct under the tax code. This is called planning.

Why do W-2 earners fail? Because they don't plan. They don't engage in tax-favorable transactions. They wait until what they call "tax season" and "refund shop," meaning they go around to several preparers to solicit the largest refund, which is a dangerous game. They also tend to compare other's returns to theirs. This is very common. "My neighbor got back $15,000, how come I only got back $2,500?" Because your neighbor has different aspects of their tax return. The *bragging* is the end result of transactions they engaged in during the year. Sure, they may have the same mortgage and property taxes as you. Maybe even the same amount of kids. However, they may have business activities or even rental properties. They may have losses from stocks they sold. The outward appearance of one's finances is not a good indicator of what you would have. Stop comparing and stop preparer shopping. Eyes on your own paper!

Let's recap with a visual. I want to drill this into your head before we move any further.

The W-2 icon represents your paycheck, whether it's through your employer or your own business from which you pay yourself. That money—outside of current living expenses and hopefully your emergency fund of savings—should be going toward your investment into business ownership and/or real estate.

I'll again use my example with the visual as it may retain better. I used my employer earnings (ordinary income from W-2) to invest in The Moneynista LLC (my business) and my first rental property. I should note that I used my retirement funds, savings, and HELOC. Many of you have access to all these things. Remember, I got educated on how to purchase investment property first. Then, with the proceeds of my business, I pay myself a salary (we will get into that later when we break down business structure). I now have ordinary income again. I use that money to funnel back into my business and rental activities. This is where I plan. Remember replacing that bathroom vanity in a rental or increasing my advertising budget, etc.?

Does this mean you have no money in the bank? Do you have to spend your whole paycheck? No. This means that you have to transition heavily taxed income into non-taxable income. The income you make can be yours physically but not taxable to Uncle Sam. This is what I mean when I say never leave ordinary income on the table. It is at the very bottom of the tax code hierarchy because it will keep you paycheck to paycheck. It's the worst income to rely on. *No one has ever become financially free from a paycheck—certainly not your average American.*

When I encourage a shift of income, people often say, "I don't have it," because it's their way of not taking accountability and responsibility. Here is a list of the resources I used to start my now multimillion-dollar business:

- **Domain Name:** GoDaddy.com, $36 for two years
- **Web Hosting:** Squarespace, $23/mo.
- **Graphic design:** Canva, free (Pro Version $119/yr.)
- **Email List:** Mailchimp, $20/mo. standard plan
- **Social Media:** Instagram, Facebook, and YouTube, free

This translates to well under $600 for the first year. The average tax refund is $2,500. How much do you spend on DoorDash or Uber Eats? I don't say this to shame you but to give you some perspective! That $600 is tax-deductible. My Instagram boosts, which were a paid expense, were tax-deductible. All of this offset my tax liability as well. Business ownership is much easier to start than investing in real estate because the start-up costs—on average, for the small business owner—are far less.

The truth is that you may spend more time watching Netflix and TikTok than building your own cash-flowing activity. You may not want to touch your savings, but inflation touches your savings every day. Chances are, you do have the time, and you do have the money. Not only that, you have the money because the money is already coming out of your paycheck, right? If you get your pay stub bi-weekly or weekly, if you look at the FICA withholdings, your federal withholdings, you're spending the money anyway. Tell Uncle Sam you want it back when you file your tax return by engaging in these activities.

Would you rather give Uncle Sam that 24% or 28% on top of state and local taxes, or would you rather put that money into your own business to grow? Even if you don't succeed by your own measures, you succeed because you still didn't give it to Uncle Sam. You gave it to yourself to try. Either way, the money is not going to stay in your bank account. That is the psychological warfare that goes on in the middle class.

The money is not in your account, and what little you can save is depreciating with inflation. Tax season is every single day, so you've got to work daily to think about what money you're giving to Uncle Sam as a W-2 earner because it's already coming out of your check.

That's what I did. I worked for my money to come back out of my withholdings via a tax refund because it is my money. Gross income is your income. It's just Uncle Sam saying, "Well, you're not going to do anything with it, so we're going to take it and invest it how we want. You're not going to provide business activities. You're not going to pump money into the economy, so we're going to take it and pump money into the economy. We're going to use it for what we deem useful." A lot of people don't agree. So if you don't agree with what they use the money for, you use it.

It's yours. Use it. You'd be surprised how many people want your product or services. If you're communicative, articulate, and knowledgeable, if you're a professional, you'll surely build a client base. Many people feel like no one will come to them, but we live in a global economy. It took me a little over a year to build up over 100,000 followers on Instagram. That's how fast business and the world travel.

Don't let procrastination and self-imposed roadblocks hinder you. You'll never get anywhere if you humdrum through life, allowing your withholdings to go uninvested. You need to invest your own withholdings. They don't have to stay with the government permanently.

I've saved well over half a million dollars in taxes by engaging in business and real estate. Business ownership also allows me to fund my retirement at three times the rate of the average employee. We'll discuss specifics on deductions and strategies later, but I can control my tax liability through expensing. More importantly, I provide valuable service to my consumers. I wouldn't encourage anyone to start a business they're not knowledgeable and passionate about, as the end goal is to provide value to your customers.

On average, my students save upwards of $30,000 in taxes per year, far more than they paid to be a lifetime member of "Tax Strategies Mastermind." They are small business owners, startups, real estate investors, and former W-2 earners who converted into wealth builders through the tax code.

The tax code is a business in and of itself. Start that business. If you've already started, go harder. I'll provide a checklist in Chapter 5 when we discuss defining your business activities.

We'll break this down into two parts: Business Ownership (non-real estate activities) and Business Activities in the form of real estate investment. Both are considered businesses by the tax code but have different standards and strategies. Before we get into each, let's start with the four tax codes you need to succeed.

CHAPTER 3

The Four Tax Codes You Need to Succeed

The tax code is over 75,000 pages. Do you need to know the whole tax code? No. The reality is you only need four codes. I am a former revenue agent in the Large Business and International Division of the IRS. My daily duties were to examine large entities that reported $10 million or more in gross receipts (income) or assets. Those corporations were usually complex and had multiple layers of operations. They had tax departments specializing in certain complex tax codes. They also had tax attorneys on retainer and whole departments in large accounting firms that handled tax matters, including audits. Luckily for the average business owner, you don't need to be well-versed in all the tax codes. I teach four codes thoroughly for the success of business owners and real estate investors. Let's go through each of them in detail, but before we do, I want to outline a very important topic: the difference between tax avoidance and tax evasion, straight off the IRS website.

- **Tax Avoidance:** "An action taken to lessen tax liability and maximize after-tax income."
- **Tax Evasion:** "The failure to pay or a deliberate underpayment of taxes."

Tax avoidance can be taking legal deductions for your business to decrease your tax liability. Tax evasion is artificially deflating your tax liability by omitting taxable income or overstating expenses. Another example is simply not filing your tax return.

Here, we teach legal tax avoidance. Let's get into each of the codes.

SECTION 6001: BOOKS & RECORDS

This section "Provides that every person liable for any tax imposed by the Code, or for the collection thereof, must keep such records, render such statements, make such returns, and comply with such rules and regulations as the Secretary may from time to time prescribe."

This simply means that you must maintain an account of all your transactions in your business activities, including real estate. This means receipts, invoices, contracts, and even correspondence in many cases.

Books and records (simply referred to as recordkeeping) are the most important part of the tax codes. If you don't have proof, it didn't happen. That's how the IRS sees things. Lack of appropriate recordkeeping can cause an IRS Examiner to remove all your deductions and tax your income. Why? Because they can classify what you do as a hobby. Hobby expenses are not allowed and, therefore, are not deductible.

Expenses

When business owners are starting their journey, this is where they make the biggest mistake. How many of you use every credit card in your wallet when paying for business expenses? If an examiner looked at those credit card statements, would they see personal expenses as well as business expenses? This is cause for concern. Your business transactions should be separate from personal transactions. This is considered appropriate. If you were ever in a federal audit of your business, the examiner most certainly would not sift through a year's worth of six or seven credit card statements. It's your job to maintain easy and clear records. So, if you are guilty of commingling your personal and business expenses, stop immediately. Dedicate a credit card to your business and use that one only for business expenses. It is easier for your accountant, easier for you, and easy for an auditor sifting through your expenses.

Income

As with business expenses, business income should not be commingled with personal income. As a business owner, you must have a dedicated business bank account. That bank account should be linked to every and any form of payment you accept. That is where all your business income should be deposited. Again, this makes it easy for you, your accountant, and an auditor to track things. There have been cases where small business owners' expenses have been disallowed because they did not have a business bank account. Now, this does not apply to real estate investors. We will talk about that in Chapter 6.

Keeping clean books and records readily available can help you manage your tax liability. How do I teach this in Mastermind? Every business must be separate from other businesses you may have and your personal activities. This way, at the end of every month, you can download your transactions from both your credit card for expenses and bank account for income every month. It's easy to sort and add in Microsoft Excel. If everything is in one place, it's easy to manage. We don't need QuickBooks or any other fancy software. Again, this does not apply to real estate. You don't need a business bank account for real estate investment. However, you need to dedicate an account for your income and a credit card for your expenses. There are also apps that manage real estate, like Stessa. All of your income and expenses are recorded in real time. This is specifically for people who manage multiple properties.

For my business owners (not real estate), once you download your activities for each month, sort them by description so all items are grouped together. Then, you can use the sum formula. This is a simple and easy way to keep books and records, and I guarantee your accountant or auditor will be quite impressed. If they ask for further information, you can just download your credit card and bank statements for the year, and they will find the corresponding expenses on your Microsoft Excel sheet. The Microsoft Excel sheet with all your transactions for each month is called a **general ledger**. Simply put, a general ledger is a record of all of a company's transactions, also known as books and records.

Here is an example of what your general ledger might look like as a student in "Tax Strategies Mastermind:"

Date	Description	Account #	Amount	Extended Details	Appears On Your Statement As	Address	City/State	Zip
02/07/2022	FACEBK *6DTHZDBXD2 FB.ME/ADS CA		900.00	P5019645868 FACEBOOK ADVERTISING FACEBK *6DTHZDBXD2 FB.ME/ADS	FACEBK *6DTHZDBXD2 FB.ME/ADS CA	1 HACKER WAY	MENLO PARK CA	94025
02/28/2022	FACEBK *9PK5SBFWD2 FB.ME/ADS CA		114.80	P4770145956 FACEBOOK ADVERTISING FACEBK *9PK5SBFWD2 FB.ME/ADS	FACEBK *9PK5SBFWD2 FB.ME/ADS CA	1 HACKER WAY	MENLO PARK CA	94025
02/10/2022	FACEBK *JD6EMCBWD2 FB.ME/ADS CA		900.00	P4865455416 FACEBOOK ADVERTISING FACEBK *JD6EMCBWD2 FB.ME/ADS	FACEBK *JD6EMCBWD2 FB.ME/ADS CA	1 HACKER WAY	MENLO PARK CA	94025
02/12/2022	FACEBK *SDFTPCBWD2 FB.ME/ADS CA		900.00	P4873896616 FACEBOOK ADVERTISING FACEBK *SDFTPCBWD2 FB.ME/ADS	FACEBK *SDFTPCBWD2 FB.ME/ADS CA	1 HACKER WAY	MENLO PARK CA	94025
02/05/2022	FACEBK *THZQRBKWD2 FB.ME/ADS CA		900.00	P4768773216 FACEBOOK ADVERTISING FACEBK *THZQRBKWD2 FB.ME/ADS	FACEBK *THZQRBKWD2 FB.ME/ADS CA	1 HACKER WAY	MENLO PARK CA	94025
02/11/2022	FACEBK*275HPB7ED2 MENLO PARK		175.00	P4760921400 ADVERTISING SERVICE FACEBK*275HPB7ED2 MENLO PARK	FACEBK*275HPB7ED2 MENLO PARK	1 HACKER WAY	MENLO PARK CA	94025
02/04/2022	FACEBK*2Z8ES83ED2 MENLO PARK		10.00	P4771092493 ADVERTISING SERVICE FACEBK*2Z8ES83ED2 MENLO PARK	FACEBK*2Z8ES83ED2 MENLO PARK	1 HACKER WAY	MENLO PARK CA	94025
02/05/2022	FACEBK*4D5THB7ED2 MENLO PARK		15.00	P4741144476 ADVERTISING SERVICE FACEBK*4D5THB7ED2 MENLO PARK P4675835765 ADVERTISING SERVICE	FACEBK*4D5THB7ED2 MENLO PARK	1 HACKER WAY	MENLO PARK CA	94025

| January | February | March | April | May | June | July | August | September | October | November | December | Total |

At the bottom, you will notice a tab for each month. Every month, you will download, sort, and add your transactions for your expenses. Simply total your expenses at the bottom, which again is a function of Microsoft Excel's sum function.

You would do the same for your income. You can keep a separate ledger of all your transactions for income, or you can simply add each month's income and place it on the same Excel sheet as your expenses. The end result would be the total amount for your expenses each month and the total income for each month. What is that called? Your **Profit & Loss statement** (P&L). Simply put:

Income - Expenses = Profit (Loss)

Has anyone ever asked for your profit and loss statement—or your P&L and you panicked? By keeping your records every month, you will always have your updated P&L statement. This whole process is crucial in maintaining your legitimacy with the IRS in the form of compliance with Section 6001 bookkeeping standards, *and* it helps you analyze your business finances. You can see where all your money is going, and you also can manage your tax liability. In "Tax Strategies Mastermind," without this step, the course is useless. I don't care about throwing content at you. I care about you executing the content taught. This is the foundation of planning. You can't manage your tax liability without the actual numbers!

What do we do with these numbers every month? As you noticed, there is a "Total" tab in the picture. It's important to keep a running total throughout the year. That's the numbers you need. For example, if you are in the month of June, your ledger should be complete with January through May tabs, with a total tab that sums up all months, again a function of Microsoft Excel's sum tool. That's where you will get your latest numbers and show your latest profit and loss statement.

That "Total" tab contains the numbers we input into over-the-counter software. We use TurboTax. I know what you're thinking: *How can we use software for the latest filing year in the current year?* Because we are planning. The items that change in the tax code, like standard deductions, don't apply to us wealth builders, you and I. We aren't standard filers. We are businesses and real estate investors. The software is accurate for each year, with minor changes that can be adjusted while planning.

Below is an illustration of how we actively manage our tax liability throughout the year:

By maintaining our financial transactions every month, we can actively manage our tax liability. Without this step, there's no point.

SECTION 162: TRADE OR BUSINESS EXPENSES

This section allows a deduction for all the ordinary and necessary expenses paid or incurred during the taxable year in carrying on any trade or business. Section 262, however, provides that no deduction is allowed for personal, living, or family expenses.

Before we dive in, let's look at some key terms that many overlook. Remember, I am a former examiner. I'm always going to teach from an audit prevention perspective, things that many gloss over that can be detrimental.

- **Ordinary:** "An ordinary expense is one that is common and accepted in your industry."
- **Necessary:** "A necessary expense is one that is helpful and appropriate for your trade or business. An expense does not have to be indispensable to be considered necessary."

This is directly from the IRS website. Let's direct our attention to the second portion of the definition of necessary. An expense does not have to be indispensable to be considered necessary. Indispensable, by definition, means absolutely necessary. In other words, I don't have to spend $10,000 on a professional website developer, but I chose to, and because it is for my business, it is, in fact, tax-deductible.

> **Pro tip:** If you are ever in an audit and an examiner contests/disallows the amount you spend on an ordinary business expense because it's a large amount, you can point out the information from the IRS website about an expense not being required to be indispensable. You can also reference Publication 535 - Business Expenses (page 3).

Now that we have those two terms out of the way, let's get into the common deductions, including the gray area. The best way to tackle this is exactly how it's listed on a business tax return.

Owner's Compensation (Only on S-Corp Tax Returns)

This is simply the salary you pay yourself as an employee and owner of your business. This can only be done if you are an S-corp. We dive into business structures in the next chapter. You will not see this line item on a Schedule C, including single-member LLCs, or partnership returns, including multi-member LLCs, as the members and owners in these structures cannot pay themselves a salary.

Owners of S-corps must pay themselves a *reasonable* salary. Reasonable by IRS standards is "the value that would ordinarily be paid for like services by like enterprises under like circumstances."

Paying yourself as an owner of your business is a sensitive audit item that could put you in financial trouble. As discussed in the next chapter, S-corps are one of two entities (including C-corps) in which the owners *must* pay themselves a salary. Why? Because these entities do not pay self-employment tax. Instead, the owners are on salary and pay employer taxes. Unlike self-employment tax, employer taxes are tax-deductible to the business, which lowers the taxable income of the entity and owners. Many business owners designate S-corp status to avoid self-employment taxes, only to wind up not being able to pay themselves a reasonable salary. The IRS sees this as tax evasion, and if ever audited, they will revoke your S-corp status and you will pay back self-employment taxes if they deem your salary as the owner unreasonable.

There is a formula we teach for determining if you can, as the owner of an S-corp, afford to pay yourself a salary. We use BizStats.com, a site that provides business statistics and financial ratios. If you don't know if you should designate S-corp status as a business owner to pay yourself a salary (which is also deductible to your business as an expense), simply go to BizStats.com. Choose S-corp in the top menu items. Choose your industry. You will get an image of an income statement with applicable percentages next to each line item. That percentage represents the item as a percentage of sales. For example, if you choose "Professional, scientific, and technical services" and next to "Compensation of Officers," the percentage is 10%, then your salary should be 10% of your sales. Let's go even further. Say your sales are $300,000. Your salary would be $30,000. If your sales were $100,000, your salary would be $10,000. This may be considered a flag in an audit, as $10,000 is relatively low for an owner's salary on average. In this case, you may not want to designate S-corp status. Again, we will talk more about S-corps in the next chapter when we discuss business structures.

The Strategy

Ultimately, you want to get to a place where you can afford to pay yourself a reasonable salary as the owner of an S-corp. This avoids self-employment tax, which is not tax-deductible, and allows you to receive compensation as an owner. As an owner, you can also contribute to a retirement plan designated for business owners. We will talk about that in the pension and profit-sharing plans section. Let's just say it's a huge strategy. More importantly, your employer taxes are deductible, unlike self-employment tax.

Salaries and Wages

This is the compensation of non-owners. Perhaps you hired a full-time administrative assistant. She/he is on the payroll. They are employees. Maybe you hired your children to work in your business. We will talk more about this strategy next, but before we do, we have to address any potential audit issues. It's vital not to confuse an employee with an independent contractor. Employees are on payroll and usually receive benefits. They also have taxes withheld from their paychecks and remitted to the government by their employer on their behalf. Ever look at your pay stub? All those taxes withheld were done by your employer and remitted to the government for you each pay period. Your employer also pays employer taxes for having you as an employee, as you would have to pay if you became the employer of an individual.

Why is it important to classify employees and contractors correctly? Simply put, many small businesses don't want to pay employer taxes. It's easier and cheaper to pay the individual outside of payroll and issue a 1099-NEC for compensation the individual received from the employer. The employer deducts that amount from their business income and pays no employer taxes. It's a win-win for the employer.

The problem is the IRS comes down hard on entities that try to classify employees as independent contractors to avoid employer taxes.

So, what makes an employee versus a contractor?

- How often does this person work for you?
- Do you set the person's schedule?

- Do you instruct or supervise the worker?
- If additional workers are needed for a job, who hires them?
- Who pays the costs related to the work?
- Is the worker economically dependent on your business?
- Does this worker make decisions that impact their own profits and losses?
- Is this person hired to work indefinitely or for a specific project or time period?
- Are the person's activities a core part of your day-to-day business?

If you, as the business owner, control most aspects of the individual, and they are an integral part of your day-to-day operations, year-to-year, the IRS may see this as an opportunity to reclassify the hired individual as an employee. What happens next? The IRS will now calculate all back employer taxes owed plus any penalties and interest.

Independent contractors receive a 1099-NEC for the total amounts paid to them. They are not employees. They are paid a set amount, and no taxes are withheld from them. They are responsible for paying taxes on their earnings on their own, and no employer taxes are paid by the employer. It is also important to note that if you are going to hire an independent contractor, using a payroll company is a fail-safe. What normally happens is that small business owners or even real estate investors who hire contractors for work engage the individual, pay the individual, and when it comes time to issue a 1099-NEC, they can't find that contractor. They don't have any information like their Social Security number, taxpayer identification number (TIN), or address. This is bad. Why? Because that contractor is long gone. They don't want to pay tax on the money you paid them, so they don't want the 1099 issued to them. In turn, taking the deduction on your business tax return for what you paid them is risky because you are required to issue them a 1099-NEC and file it with the IRS.

If you use a payroll company, upon hiring the contractor, whether it's for business or real estate, they are forced to fill out the correct information electronically with your payroll provider. So when it comes time to file the tax return and take the deduction, you have legitimate documentation. The payroll company will file the 1099-NEC for you to the IRS and issue the 1099-NEC to the contractor you hired. Again, this is done *before* you actually engage in the relationship.

A common mistake many business owners and real estate investors make: They hire someone to do a short-term job, a contractor. The job is performed without registering them in the payroll platform. Therefore, they do not get the information necessary to take the deduction for the expense. Now you can't issue the 1099 to take the deduction. You are also non-compliant with the tax code.

Example: I found a contractor to do repair work on a rental. I sent them a link via my payroll company to fill out the information to be set up as a contractor in my employer portal. He was sent a link to his email to fill out a Form W-9, a Request for Taxpayer Identification Number and Certification. (See below for an example.) This must be filled out by the contractor *before* you engage in their services. You can easily download this form from the IRS website, but again, the payroll company will handle this. Automation is key. Don't do anything manually. When my contractor was done with the job, I logged into my payroll portal and set up payment according to his invoice. The info is held in my payroll portal for end-of-year reporting. I don't have to worry about deadlines for filing or lack of documentation and certainly non-compliance, as any payment of $600 or more requires a 1099 to the recipient.

The only time you don't have to issue a 1099-NEC to a hired contractor is when they accept online payments via a third-party processor, in which you can use your business credit card to pay for the job. When they have a third-party payment processor in which you use your credit card to pay, that is receipt enough, and the payment processor issues its own 1099 to the contractor, so the responsibility of reporting the income is now on that payment processor. Examples are Square, Stripe, or any platform that takes credit card payments. Contractors who want to be paid cash or direct deposit from your bank account need to be set up on your payroll platform, and it's fairly easy to do. Below is what the contractor would receive every January for the prior year from you as the employer.

[Form 1099-NEC (Rev. January 2024) — Nonemployee Compensation, Copy 1 For State Tax Department]

Now, let's talk about strategy.

How is most generational wealth built? Not only by moving within the tax code but also by including the "generation" in generational wealth: your kids, your spouse, etc. You can absolutely hire your children in your business. The IRS has a whole page dedicated to parents who hire their children in their business. You can hire your nephew, niece, grandmother, grandfather, or next-door neighbor. For the purposes of this strategy, let's focus on your kids. There are two main criteria for hiring your children (or anyone related to you, for that matter). The job must be:

- **Bona Fide (real/genuine):** It must make sense for your business and be a real position.

- **Compensation has to be reasonable:** Just like your compensation as the owner must be reasonable. This means you are paying them what you would pay anyone unrelated to you for the job they are doing.

What are some jobs that kids can do to be considered genuine? Social media content creators, clerical jobs, courier duties. These make sense for kids. Remember, they must be on payroll, which means they receive a paycheck. If you issue a 1099, they may be subject to self-employment taxes.

Does the age of the child matter? Absolutely. You must adhere to the federal Department of Labor laws and the Department of Labor laws in your state. For the most part, if your child is at least 14 years of age, you are in the clear, but be sure to go to the Department of Labor for your state. They also cannot be full-time if they are underage. They must be part-time.

What if your child is under 14 years of age? There are rules for children on the Department of Labor website, both federal and for your particular state. Make sure you visit the U.S. Department of Labor's YouthRules.gov website. Click on "Young Workers" and you can select the age of your child for applicable rules. Be sure to click the link for your state rules as well by visiting your state Department of Labor website.

So now that we have established that your teen or pre-teen is eligible to work for you under U.S. Department of Labor laws and your state laws, you will decide if they are an employee or contractor. Is your child working every day after school? Are they working on a consistent basis? Are their duties one-off, like creating content for your social media page for a month, or is it ongoing as their main task daily?

If they are an employee, like any other individual you hire classified as an employee, you must put them on payroll. This involves hiring a payroll company. You absolutely must outsource this function as a small business owner. There are plenty of small business payroll companies to choose from, such as ADP and Gusto. The payroll companies do all the math and all the work. All you have to do is add a new hire as an employee or contractor. Why is a payroll company important? As a business owner, you are responsible for remitting the correct amount of taxes to the government. You are responsible not only for issuing 1099s to your contractors but also for filing your employer-issued 1099s with the IRS and issuing W-2s by January 31 of every year. There is a penalty for filing your 1099s late.

A payroll company will usually handle all your filing deadlines for you. These include your annual Form 940, which is your Employer's Annual Federal Unemployment (FUTA) Tax Return, and 941s, which are quarterly employer federal tax returns that report income taxes, Social Security tax, or Medicare tax withheld from employees' paychecks. They'll also pay the employer's portion of Social Security or Medicare tax. Don't get too worked up in this detail. Selecting a payroll company is your *only* job. Add your business bank account and any standard information like name and address of business, etc. After that, your job is to add any new hires as either employees or independent contractors with their fixed or recurring pay. The payroll company will do the rest. You can set payroll to be recurring or run it manually, which means you dictate when the employee is paid. This usually works well when your children work in your business.

Let's talk about tax strategy when hiring your children. You can pay your kids up to the standard deduction for single filers per year, and they will have no federal tax liability. They must be on the payroll, not 1099. As stated several times throughout this book, they will be subject to self-employment tax. What does this do? Their pay is an expense to your business, which reduces your taxable income. They now have tax-free money to invest, possibly in a Roth IRA. A Roth IRA can be started at any age. We will dive into retirement separately in this section. Now, imagine starting your 12-year-old in a Roth IRA. They would have a lot of financial flexibility by the time they are adults. You're essentially legally shifting money out of your business via the deduction of paying your child for a bona fide and reasonably compensated job. That money is tax-free to them, and they can invest it at an early age. This is a trifecta of wealth building (see the diagram below).

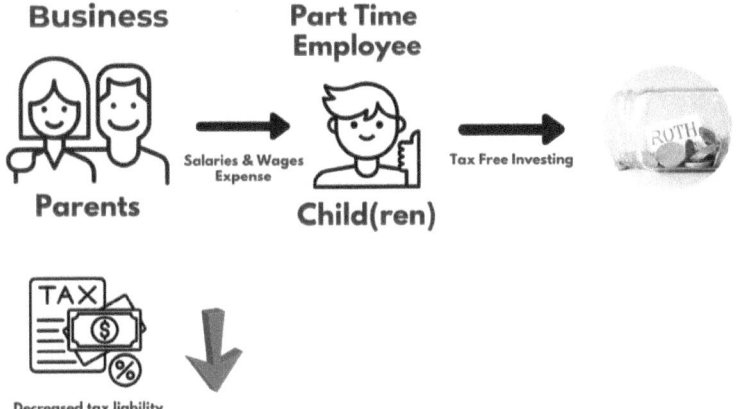

We will talk about the expansion of this strategy in the pension and profit-sharing plans below and include the owner's compensation. For now, let's stay in order of the tax return.

Repairs and Maintenance

This deduction is pretty much self-explanatory. It usually applies if your business has to have a physical location. Let's say you have an office where you conduct your business activities. The bathroom for your clients becomes out of service due to plumbing issues. You need to call a plumber. The plumber comes and fixes any issues. That expense is deductible to your business. Just as a note from a former examiner in the IRS, please have any and all invoices for your business in your actual business name. Pay any and all expenses with your business credit card or bank account. Try not to have any business expenses in your personal name.

Bad Debts

Bad debts are simply amounts owed to your business by customers. If you cannot collect funds owed to you, they are deductible under bad debts. This is not typical in today's average business. This applies to corporations that use the accrual-based method of accounting. Income is recognized when earned, and not received yet, and expenses are recognized when incurred and not yet paid. Most small businesses operate on a cash basis. Income is recognized when received, and expenses are recognized when paid.

In instances of accrual-based accounting for corporations, usually the business is quoted for a service or offered a product with a price tag, and neither is received until payment is made and received. However, you may have some businesses that operate under an older structure under which they provide a product or a service ahead of time and bill afterward. If that payment is considered uncollectible, it's a bad debt. If you operate under this structure, you would have a bad debt policy in place. This would specifically lay out a systematic procedure to determine when the amount owed becomes uncollectible. For example, after 15 or 30 days of the due date for payment, you send out a notice reminding the customer that they have a balance. You may send another letter after 60 days. Your last and final letter may be after 90 days. Then, you can consider the debt uncollectible based on your policy.

Another instance is when a company goes bankrupt and becomes insolvent. They may not be able to pay their creditors, including you. You can then consider the debt uncollectible.

Perhaps you made a business loan. You had an actual loan agreement with loan terms and market interest rates. You received payments on the 1st of the month, including interest, for five months. That loan then went into default and the business was unable to pay you back. They went bankrupt, perhaps.

In any of these cases, the money owed is considered a bad debt and, therefore, tax-deductible. But that's not the end. You must issue a 1099-C, Cancellation of Debt. Since the entity or person who owes you is unable to pay you back, it is considered income to them. A 1099-C is required for anyone who has had debt canceled in the amount of $600 or more. See the following image of a 1099-C. Your business would be the creditor as the entity owed money.

Rents

Rent is any amount you pay for the use of property you do *not* own for use in your trade or business. An example would be leasing office space. I'm going to use office space because it's a common example and has exceptions.

Here's what you cannot expense in full: commissions, bonuses, fees, and other amounts you pay to obtain a lease on the property. These are considered capital costs. You must allocate these costs over the term of the lease.

Example: You secure a lease for five years. The broker commission is $5,000. You cannot deduct the full $5,000. You must allocate that fee over the length of the lease. $5,000 / 5 years = $1,000 a year as an expense allocated toward your rental expense for each of the five years.

Interest

For any loans taken out for your business, the interest is tax-deductible. The following conditions must be met:
- You are legally liable for that debt.
- Both you and the lender intend for the debt to be repaid.
- You and the lender have a true debtor-creditor relationship (arm's length).

I do not recommend loans between the owner and the business. These are highly audited items amongst small business owners. You have money loaned to your business called "loans *from* shareholders." Conversely, there are loans from your business called "loans *to* shareholders." Any item with two related parties, in this case, the business owner and their own business, presents a potential conflict of interest and unscrupulous transactions.

In this scenario of interest expense for your business, this would fall under a loan from a shareholder (you) in which the business would be able to deduct any interest payments made to you. You must have what is called an **arm's length transaction**. It's a fancy term for "legitimate." In other words, the loan terms, including principal amounts, must be stated with applicable interest rates. Repayment terms must be similar to an agreement that would come from a lender. You must show payment from your business to yourself on a regular and consistent basis with principal and interest easily identifiable, as only the interest is considered a deduction. Otherwise, this loan will appear illegitimate, and any interest you deduct will be disallowed.

Depreciation

This is an expense very specific to certain items. Depreciation is an expense granted to you by the tax code that is not actually paid. It accounts for normal wear and tear of business-use property while being used for business purposes. Do you run a construction business? Chances are you have heavy equipment like a crane or a bulldozer. Do you own rental properties? You have depreciation expenses. Do you have a vehicle for your business? You will also have depreciation expenses. All this means is that the asset(s) will have a useful life, and the cost of that asset will be divided by that useful life. The useful life is determined by the IRS.

Some examples are below.
- **Standard passenger vehicle:** 5 years
- **Rental property four units and under:** 27.5 years
- **Rental property five units or more:** 39 years
- **Tractors:** 3 years
- **Computers and office equipment:** 5 years

All this means is that for the number of years assigned by the IRS for the useful life, you will divide the cost of the asset by those years. An exception is rental real estate, as you have to remove the value of the land first.

Example: Let's use a rental property as an example. If you purchase a rental property with four units or less for, say, $500,000, the useful life is 27.5 years. If the land value, for example, is $50,000, you would deduct that amount from the cost. $500,000 - $50,000 = $450,000. This is called your **depreciable basis**. Now, use that number and divide it by 27.5 years: $450,000 / 27.5 years = $16,363 in depreciation expense per year. Again, this is not an expense you actually pay. It's like a "gifted" expense from the IRS for engaging in business activity or rentals. This is where most of the wealth comes from in the tax code—**phantom expenses**. It's called phantom because you don't actually pay it; you are just granted the expense as a reward, if you will, for engaging in the transaction. We will go deeper into rentals in the real estate section in Chapter 6.

Advertising

This is also self-explanatory. This is an activity to promote awareness about your product or service for sale. Advertising and marketing are important activities that many business owners undervalue. This activity alone tells the IRS you have the intent to make a profit. This is part of solidifying yourself as a business and not a hobby. When your advertising or marketing expenses are relatively low, it speaks to minimal involvement and participation. In fact, I find most business owners hinder their profitability by not focusing on advertising. Remember my paid Instagram boosts? That's part of my intent to profit.

I am promoting awareness of my brand. I also ran Facebook and Instagram ads. This translates to non-hobby activities.

Pension and Profit-Sharing Plans

Many business owners overlook a huge strategy in retirement planning. As an employee of your current employer, you are usually offered the standard 401(k) or something similar. (For me, it was called a "Thrift Savings Plan" as a federal government employee.) Usually, the maximum you can contribute to your employer-sponsored retirement plan in a year is, in comparison, minimal to your options as a business owner. As of 2024, the maximum contribution is $23,000. You may have employer matching, which is great, but did you know the retirement plan options for business owners can be far greater? Let's talk about the different retirement plan options for business owners, *as this is another huge move for wealth in the tax code.*

SIMPLE IRA: Savings Incentive Match Plan for Employees, better referred to as a SIMPLE IRA, has the following criteria:
- Employers with 100 or fewer employees
- Employee and Employer contributions

To be eligible for a SIMPLE IRA, an employee must have received at least $5,000 in compensation in the previous two calendar years and expect to receive at least that much in the present calendar year.

The IRS requires that the employer make a contribution on behalf of the employee. This can be either a dollar-for-dollar match of up to 3% of their salary or a flat 2% of pay. Employers must contribute regardless of whether the employee elects to.

SEP IRA: Simplified Employee Pension, also referred to as a SEP IRA, is one of my favorite plans for single-owner businesses where *the only employee is the owner*, particularly single-owner S-corps. This is not optimal if you have other employees.

If you have employees, they are eligible for SEP contributions. The requirements for eligibility are:

1. At least 21 years of age
2. Has performed service for you in at least three of the immediately preceding five years
3. Received the minimum compensation from your business in the tax year ($750 in 2024 and 2023, $650 in 2022 and 2021, for example). You can easily Google this information every year.

None of your employees make their own contributions. You, as the employer, must make *all* the contributions on behalf of your employees. If you have adult children working for you, this may be a great strategy to build their retirement faster than the average American employee. Why? Because the maximum contribution is three times more than the average employer-sponsored plan. For 2024, the maximum contribution to a SEP IRA for a business owner is $69,000 or 25% of compensation, whichever is *lower*. The same goes for the employees of your business.

For example, if you own a business and pay yourself, as the owner of an S corporation, a salary of $100,000, you may contribute $25,000 (25%) to your SEP. If you employ your adult child (21 years or older) who works full-time (minors cannot work full-time under Department of Labor laws) a salary of $50,000, you, as the employer, must contribute $12,500 (25%) for the year on their behalf. They do not have to contribute. If you do extremely well in your business and are able to compensate for, say, $300,000, 25% of that salary is $75,000, but the limit for the year 2024 is $69,000, so you may contribute the maximum amount of $69,000. This works well as your business grows.

If you have several employees, this may be an expense you do not want to take on, so as I said, it works well as a sole owner of the business or if you want to employ your adult child(ren).

This kind of retirement plan is a huge wealth-building tool. The contribution limits each year are almost always three times higher than a regular employer-sponsored plan.

Solo 401(k): This is for businesses in which you are the only employee or where the only employee is your spouse. This works similarly to a SEP IRA, except you cannot have any additional employees other than yourself and your spouse. The contribution limits are the same for the most part; however, the Solo 401(k) is a bit more complex than a SEP in that it can take longer to set up, but you can typically borrow from a Solo 401(k), unlike a SEP. You can generally borrow up to $50,000 per year or 50% of the balance, whichever is *less*.

So now that we've looked at the basic retirement plans for businesses, let's talk strategy again, still with generational wealth in mind. That means your children or other family members. We will illustrate children in this example.

Remember our prior example where you paid your child a salary, and that salary was a deductible expense? In turn, your minor child was able to contribute to a Roth IRA at an early age. Let's add the component of retirement. I'm going to use the maximum contributions for illustrative purposes.

If you are a business owner who has designated S-corp, meaning you can afford to pay yourself a salary as the owner in addition to paying employees, you can now open up a retirement plan, depending on your employee structure. Let's say it's just you, your spouse, and your adult child who is at least 21 years of age who's involved in the family business.

You and your spouse will contribute to your retirement plan. Both can contribute up to the maximum. For 2024, it's $69,000. Because your business is doing extremely well, you can maximize your contributions, so you open a SEP IRA because your adult child is your employee—remember, Solo 401(k) does not allow employees outside of spouses. You are able to contribute the full $69,000 to your and your spouse's retirement due to your compensation, and you are required to contribute up to 25% or $69,000 to your adult child employee as well. Perhaps you pay them $100,000 a year. So you can contribute up to $25,000 to their retirement. Remember, your company makes all the contributions directly from your business bank account, not payroll earnings.

The net effect is that you are able to reduce your taxable income by all of the contributions to the retirement plan. In this case, $163,000 (you and your spouse's full contributions of $69,000 each and your adult child employee of $25,000). Don't forget your child(ren) must be employees (W-2), not contractors (1099). See the visual illustration below.

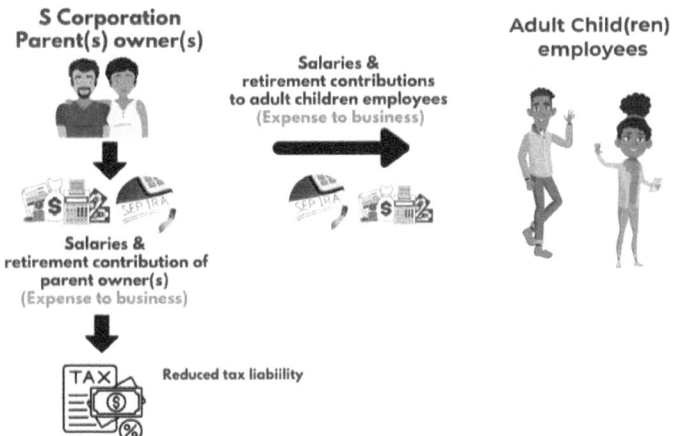

This also works for minor children as well. Remember, you must adhere to child labor laws, so refer to the U.S. Department of Labor and your state's Department of Labor. Since the goal here is to start your children building wealth quite young, let's pretend they are not adults, and you have to adhere to Department of Labor guidelines. They are part-time employees in this case.

SECURE Act 401(k) Rules for Part-Time Employees: Although not required, an employer could choose to let part-time employees share in employer contributions. Plans can require less than 1,000 hours in a 12-month period to participate. Part-timers working 500–999 hours can participate.

Your retirement contributions and your contributions to your minor child's retirement plan are tax-deductible to your business as well. They cannot have SEP contributions as they are not at least 21 years of age. So, you may opt for a traditional employer-sponsored plan for them.

The overall picture is that, as an owner rather than an employee, you can grow your retirement fund exponentially compared to most Americans. Imagine contributing up to $69,000-plus every year (assuming you meet the compensation requirements). How much would you have for retirement in contrast to most Americans? *This is also where the wealthy secure their future financially.* They are not contributing like employees. They are contributing as owners. Their children are contributing at early ages, building before adult years many times. Isn't that generational wealth?

Other Deductions

This captures many other items that are not specifically labeled on the tax return. Let's go through the most common and most effective.

Travel: Deductible travel expenses include:
- Air, train, bus, or your own vehicle
- Hotel/motel expenses for business
- Rental car expenses while out of town on business
- Taxi, shuttle fares while out of town on business
- Gas, oil, parking fees, and tolls while out of town on business

Keep *all* receipts, and remember, use that dedicated business credit card, not your personal card. If you don't have a business credit card, get one! It sounds harsh, but an IRS Examiner may not care about your personal circumstances. Personal credit cards equal personal expenses in their eyes.

I'm going to address what many small business owners attempt—commingling personal travel with business. You cannot take a trip to Disney with the family, work for an hour or two a day, and classify any part of the trip as business. *Don't do it.* Keep business business and personal personal. This is not something you want to debate with an IRS Examiner. You will almost certainly lose.

Meals & Entertainment: As of 2023, deductions are now back where they were before 2021. The majority of business meals are now 50% deductible instead of 100%, and entertainment expenses are not deductible at all.

Sorry, those basketball tickets are not deductible, even if you're trying to obtain a client.

Home Office Deduction: This is a common one. If you dedicate a space in your home to conduct business, you can deduct a portion of the expenses that come with that office.

Your home office qualifies as your principal place of business if you meet the following requirements:

- You use the office exclusively and regularly for administrative or management activities of your trade or business.
- You have no other fixed location where you conduct substantial administrative or management activities of your trade or business.

This requires some math. You need the total square footage of your home—whether you rent or own doesn't matter. You also need the total square footage of your office space.

Example: You live in a 1,000-square-foot home and your office space in your home is 200 square feet. Your deduction for all expenses of your home would be 20% (200/1,000) as your office space is 20% of your home. If your mortgage or rent is $2,000/mo., your deductible portion would be $400 (20%) per month or $4,800 per year. The same applies to your utilities and property taxes, if applicable. Please keep all your utility bills for the year handy and your rental agreement if you rent. Most bills are paperless these days, so you can keep a folder on your computer, preferably an external server like iCloud. *Documentation is everything.*

SECTION 179: ELECTION TO EXPENSE ITEMS NORMALLY CAPITALIZED

Before we get into Section 179, I want to use the standard example of a vehicle used for business. This is common among most small business owners. If you use your car only for business purposes, you may deduct its entire cost of ownership and operation (subject to limits). However, if you use the car for *both* business and personal purposes, you may deduct only the cost of its business use. You have two options for utilizing your vehicle for business purposes: standard mileage rate and actual expenses.

Standard Mileage Rate

The standard mileage rate is the cost of operating your car for business. To use the standard mileage rate, you must own or lease the car and:

- You must not operate five or more cars at the same time, as in a fleet operation.
- You must not have claimed a depreciation deduction for the car using any method other than straight-line.
- You must not have claimed a Section 179 deduction on the car.
- You must not have claimed the special depreciation allowance on the car.
- You must not have claimed actual expenses after 1997 for a car you lease.

To use the standard mileage rate for a car you own, you must choose to use it in the *first year* the car is available for use in your business. Then, in later years, you can choose to use the standard mileage rate or actual expenses.

For a car you lease, you must use the standard mileage rate method for the entire lease period (including renewals) if you choose the standard mileage rate.

Actual expenses

To use the actual expense method, you must determine what it actually costs to operate the car for the portion of the overall use of the car that's business use. Include gas, oil, repairs, tires, insurance, registration fees, licenses, and depreciation (or lease payments) attributable to the portion of the total miles driven that are business miles.

Using actual expenses, include:
- Depreciation
- Lease payments
- Gas and oil
- Tires
- Repairs and tune-ups
- Insurance
- Registration fees

Now, let's talk about Section 179. You cannot use the standard mileage rate with Section 179. This section of the tax code acts in a similar way to depreciation. Instead of taking the cost of an item over the useful life (in years), Section 179 allows you to expense a large portion of the cost in the year you purchase and **place it in service** (which means ready and available for use even if it's not in use). Section 179 property is any non-residential property, like machinery, equipment, office furniture, and business vehicles.

Again, we will use your business vehicle. Vehicles eligible for Section 179 are passenger vehicles, heavy SUVs, trucks, and vans for business-related purposes. It's important to pay attention to verbiage.

To claim a Section 179 deduction, you must:
- Purchase the vehicle for business.
- Use the vehicle for business *more than 50%* of the time.
- Only deduct the business use of the car.
- Take the deduction in the year you buy and place the vehicle in service (aka when it's "ready and available").
- Understand Section 179 limits, such as the annual deduction amount limit.
- Reduce your depreciable basis in the car by the amount of the deduction.
- Not claim the standard mileage tax deduction in the same year.

Your vehicle must have a gross vehicle weight rating (GVWR) of *at least* 6,000 pounds and *no more than* 14,000 pounds. You can find this information on the manufacturer's label inside the edge of the driver's side door, where the door hinges meet the vehicle's frame (or with a Google search). Most car dealerships are also aware of this strategy, so they can also point you in the right direction.

In addition to Section 179 for your business vehicle, you can also take depreciation. It's called "bonus depreciation" (we will dive deeper into this in the real estate tax code).

Example: let's look at the average business owner. Most of us only have one vehicle that we may use for both business and personal use. It is incumbent upon you to provide the exact percentage of time used for business via documentation. Do you keep a log of client visits? Do you log your mileage? These are things most business owners fail to do. In an audit, you will most certainly be disallowed the deduction for failing to keep proper documentation. Remember we talked about books and records? Sometimes, you need more than your finances. Keep a log of miles driven or client visits. MileIQ is a great way to keep track of mileage. Keep a separate folder for each client, customer, or tenant. *Documentation is crucial in every deduction.* Again, it is part of record-keeping, and as I pointed out at the beginning of this chapter, record-keeping is the most important task to success in the tax code.

If you are a household with two vehicles, it is a lot easier to convince an IRS Examiner that you dedicate one vehicle solely for business as you have another vehicle available for personal use. In "Tax Strategies Mastermind," we use software (TurboTax), and this question is asked when inputting information about your vehicle.

I cannot overstate the importance of documentation and organization. Messiness in your recordkeeping is very dangerous. It's also important that I warn you to keep business activities separate from personal. This is usually very difficult for the average person trying to maneuver, but it will save you a headache in all aspects of maintaining your business and its legitimacy, not only with the IRS but with a lender or investors you may want to pitch to. I'm very adamant about not commingling any finances or activities. I will give you some examples in the next and final tax code you need to know.

SECTION 469: PASSIVE ACTIVITY LOSSES (REAL ESTATE)

The last tax code you need to know—and it's super-important—relates to real estate.

Real estate is one of the most powerful wealth-building avenues you can take. Unlike business ownership, you don't have to love it, but you do have to utilize it if you want to exponentially build your wealth using the tax code. Most of the time, those interested in becoming real estate investors (commonly known as landlords) are focused on cash flow: the money you receive in rent minus any expenses. I have news for you—

that's not where the real wealth lies. It's in the tax benefits of investing in real estate.

Let's talk about the two types of real estate. There are single-family homeowners that actually occupy/live in the property. We will refer to them as owner-occupied.

Then there are those who purchase property for the sole purpose of renting out to others, commonly called tenants. These are real estate investors, commonly called landlords.

Let's discuss the difference between the two for tax purposes.

Single-Family Owner-Occupied

This is the typical scenario. Remember my story? I purchased my first property to live in. Although a condo, it's still considered a single occupancy unit and treated the same in the tax code because I lived there at first. On the tax return, this translates into two basic expenses that are allowed: mortgage interest and property taxes. This is located on the homeowner's schedule A itemized deductions of their individual tax return.

Rental Property (Investment)

The other type of property is the investment property. I am an investor. I rent out properties for the purpose of collecting rent from occupants, called tenants. They each have a lease agreement with fixed terms and rental rates per month. A person in this position is automatically engaged in a business activity per the tax code. You are a landlord. Your deductions are similar to a regular business tax return, except they are commonly reported on Schedule E. These deductions include the following:
- Advertising
- Auto & Travel
- Cleaning and Maintenance
- Commissions to brokers
- Insurance
- Legal and professional fees

- Management fees
- Mortgage interest
- Property taxes
- Repairs
- Supplies
- Depreciation (including bonus depreciation)

You can already see the difference between an owner-occupied property and an investment property.

The Tax Code

I won't fill your head with tax code verbiage, as it will confuse you even more. I will break it down into many parts, and we will discuss strategy in Chapter 6. It's important that you correctly understand this information.

Section 469 simply indicates that your rental activity is considered a passive activity, meaning you don't have to actually labor. You collect rent and pay the carrying costs. You can take all the deductions, but any loss created by these deductions can only offset your rental income. There are three key items that make real estate impactful:

- Depreciation
- Bonus depreciation
- Real estate professional status (REPS)

Depreciation: As you recall, depreciation is a phantom expense. This is simply an expense that the government gives you to account for normal wear and tear on your business asset—even a rental. You don't actually pay it; you are "gifted" this expense for being an investor.

Bonus Depreciation: This is similar to depreciation, except it doesn't relate to the property but the personal items and land improvements that are depreciable under a shorter life span (under 20 years). In short, it's an extra expense that's "gifted" to you for being an investor.

Real Estate Professional Status: This is simply changing your involvement in your rental activities so you can benefit from the phantom losses created by depreciation and bonus depreciation (phantom expenses). Normally, as stated, your real estate activity is considered passive. If you engage in rental activities under IRS guidelines, your activity becomes *active*, and this means that your losses can offset your W-2 (ordinary income) and even business income because it's no longer a passive activity.

These three items specifically are the wealth-building tools in the tax code for real estate.

We will go through this strategy in detail under section 469 in Chapter 6, as it deserves its own chapter, and I don't want to overwhelm you. My goal here is to identify the benefit of being an investor in the tax code, so please be sure to really pay attention to Chapter 6, which is dedicated to rental real estate.

To Recap

The four tax codes to set you up for successful wealth building are Section 6001, Section 162, Section 179, and Section 469. Now that you know the codes, let's dive into the actual business structures and what they mean.

CHAPTER 4

Business Structure

There are five business structures in the tax code (notice I didn't say tax structures). These structures are:
- **Sole Proprietorship**
- **Single-Member LLC**
- **Multi-Member LLC**
- **S Corporation**
- **C Corporation**

All entities, with the exception of the C corporation, are called "pass-through" entities. This means all profits and losses from business operations *pass through* to the owner(s)' individual tax return. These entities are not taxed separately like a C corporation. Let's talk about each and the tax aspects in detail.

SOLE PROPRIETORSHIP

A sole proprietorship is a type of enterprise that is owned and run by one person, and there is *no legal distinction* between the owner and the business entity. The owner is solely responsible for any debts and tax obligations the business accumulates.

A sole proprietor does not necessarily work "alone"—it is possible for the individual to employ other people. However, there is only one owner.

A sole proprietor reports all income or losses from their business on their respective individual tax return, Form 1040 Schedule C.

The owner cannot pay themselves a salary. This is an important note.

A sole proprietor is responsible for paying self-employment tax. This tax consists of Social Security and Medicare.

This structure does not need any formalities. You don't need to form a sole proprietorship through your secretary of state website, unlike all other entities. This is the simplest structure of all.

A sole proprietor is also responsible for paying estimated taxes quarterly.

The major disadvantage of a sole proprietorship is that the owner and the business itself are not separate and distinct. If there are any lawsuits against the owner or the business, the assets can be at risk.

You can see the diagram below of where your business operations are reported.

SCHEDULE C
(Form 1040)

Department of the Treasury
Internal Revenue Service

Profit or Loss From Business
(Sole Proprietorship)

Attach to Form 1040, 1040-SR, 1040-SS, 1040-NR, or 1041; partnerships must generally file Form 1065.

Go to *www.irs.gov/ScheduleC* for instructions and the latest information.

OMB No. 1545-0074

2023

Attachment Sequence No. 09

Name of proprietor | Social security number (SSN)

A Principal business or profession, including product or service (see instructions)

B Enter code from instructions

C Business name. If no separate business name, leave blank.

D Employer ID number (EIN) (see instr.)

E Business address (including suite or room no.)
   City, town or post office, state, and ZIP code

F Accounting method: (1) ☐ Cash (2) ☐ Accrual (3) ☐ Other (specify)

G Did you "materially participate" in the operation of this business during 2023? If "No," see instructions for limit on losses . ☐ Yes ☐ No

H If you started or acquired this business during 2023, check here . . . . ☐

I Did you make any payments in 2023 that would require you to file Form(s) 1099? See instructions . . . . . ☐ Yes ☐ No

J If "Yes," did you or will you file required Form(s) 1099? . . . . ☐ Yes ☐ No

Part I Income

1 Gross receipts or sales. See instructions for line 1 and check the box if this income was reported to you on Form W-2 and the "Statutory employee" box on that form was checked . . . . ☐ | 1
2 Returns and allowances . . . . | 2
3 Subtract line 2 from line 1 . . . . | 3
4 Cost of goods sold (from line 42) . . . . | 4
5 **Gross profit.** Subtract line 4 from line 3 . . . . | 5
6 Other income, including federal and state gasoline or fuel tax credit or refund (see instructions) . . . . | 6
7 **Gross income.** Add lines 5 and 6 . . . . | 7

Part II Expenses. Enter expenses for business use of your home **only** on line 30.

8   Advertising . . . . . . | 8 | | 18 Office expense (see instructions) . | 18
9   Car and truck expenses (see instructions) . . | 9 | | 19 Pension and profit-sharing plans . | 19
                                                        20 Rent or lease (see instructions):
10 Commissions and fees . | 10 | | a Vehicles, machinery, and equipment | 20a
11 Contract labor (see instructions) | 11 | | b Other business property . . | 20b
12 Depletion . . . . . | 12 | | 21 Repairs and maintenance . . | 21
13 Depreciation and section 179 expense deduction (not included in Part III) (see instructions) . . | 13 | | 22 Supplies (not included in Part III) . | 22
                                                        23 Taxes and licenses . . . . | 23
                                                        24 Travel and meals:
14 Employee benefit programs (other than on line 19) . | 14 | | a Travel . . . . | 24a
                                                        b Deductible meals (see instructions) | 24b
15 Insurance (other than health) | 15 | | 25 Utilities . . . . | 25
16 Interest (see instructions): | 26 Wages (less employment credits) . | 26
a   Mortgage (paid to banks, etc.) | 16a | | 27a Other expenses (from line 48) . . | 27a
b   Other . . . . . . | 16b | | b Energy efficient commercial bldgs deduction (attach Form 7205) . . | 27b
17 Legal and professional services | 17 |

28 **Total expenses** before expenses for business use of home. Add lines 8 through 27b . . . . . . ▶ | 28
29 Tentative profit or (loss). Subtract line 28 from line 7 . . . . | 29
30 Expenses for business use of your home. Do not report these expenses elsewhere. Attach Form 8829 unless using the simplified method. See instructions.
    Simplified method filers only: Enter the total square footage of (a) your home: _____
    and (b) the part of your home used for business: _____ . Use the Simplified Method Worksheet in the instructions to figure the amount to enter on line 30 . . . . | 30
31 **Net profit or (loss).** Subtract line 30 from line 29.
    • If a profit, enter on both **Schedule 1 (Form 1040), line 3,** and on **Schedule SE, line 2.** (If you checked the box on line 1, see instructions.) Estates and trusts, enter on **Form 1041, line 3.**
    • If a loss, you **must** go to line 32. | 31
32 If you have a loss, check the box that describes your investment in this activity. See instructions.
    • If you checked 32a, enter the loss on both **Schedule 1 (Form 1040), line 3,** and on **Schedule SE, line 2.** (If you checked the box on line 1, see the line 31 instructions.) Estates and trusts, enter on **Form 1041, line 3.**
    • If you checked 32b, you **must** attach **Form 6198.** Your loss may be limited. | 32a ☐ All investment is at risk.
32b ☐ Some investment is not at risk.

For Paperwork Reduction Act Notice, see the separate instructions.   Cat. No. 11334P   Schedule C (Form 1040) 2023

LIMITED LIABILITY COMPANIES (LLCs)

There are two types of Limited Liability Companies (LLCs):
- **Single-Member LLC**
- **Multi-Member LLC**

LLCs must be formed through your state's secretary of state. Usually, this can be done online.

LLCs are separate and distinct entities from their owners, referred to as members, as the title suggests. We will use "member" and "owner" interchangeably.

You will receive Articles of Organization. Articles of Organization are part of a formal legal document used to establish a limited liability company (LLC) at the state level. The materials are also used to create the rights, powers, duties, liabilities, and other obligations between each member of an LLC and also between the LLC and its members.

An operating agreement is an important document used by LLCs because it outlines the business' financial and functional decisions, including rules, regulations, and provisions. The purpose of the document is to govern the internal operations of the business in a way that suits the specific needs of the business owners.

Important items to note:
- Member(s) of an LLC cannot pay themselves a salary. They can pay employees.
- LLC members will also pay self-employment taxes like sole proprietorships.
- LLCs are pass-through entities like sole proprietorships. Everything flows through to the individual members' tax returns.

Single-Member LLC

A single-member LLC is just like a sole proprietorship with one exception: There is a legal distinction between the owner and the business. If there is a lawsuit against the business owner or the business, the claimant can only access the assets of one, while the other is protected as a separate entity.

Your single-member LLC is treated as a sole proprietorship for tax purposes and is also reported on Form 1040 Schedule C.

The transition from sole proprietor to single-member LLC should take place when you are out of the start-up phase of your business. I advise small business owners to refrain from forming any business structure through the secretary of state until they are out of the start-up phase. Why? Many individuals start something they don't finish. You're at Thanksgiving dinner with your family and decide to start a pet grooming mobile service. Everyone's all excited, and you and three of your cousins decide to be partners. Once you identify the costs of the vehicle and equipment, including installation and supplies, all three of your cousins decide they cannot participate due to other financial obligations, sudden disinterest, or lack of funds. Now, you are all alone in the venture. You either decide to continue, or you scrap the idea totally due to lack of funds or your own outside obligations. Now, your idea went from a partnership to a sole proprietorship to non-existent.

In this example, had you registered the business immediately with your secretary of state, you would have had to pay the fees for formation and any fees to dissolve the LLC. If you forgot about the LLC, you would have incurred state penalties as you are required to file a state tax return and pay the annual or biannual LLC filing fees, depending on your state of incorporation.

If you have any outstanding LLCs that are not active, my advice is to go to your secretary of state, where you formed the structure and dissolve it. There's usually a nominal fee. Make sure you filed all state returns, including the final return. Even if you have no income or expenses, you are required to file your state return.

Now that you are sure to start your business, you want to protect it and yourself by separating the two entities, you as the individual and the business entity.

Multi-Member LLCs

A multi-member LLC is simply an entity with two or more members. For tax purposes, a multi-member LLC is treated as a partnership, which is when two or more people manage and operate a business as co-owners and share in profits (and losses).

A multi-member LLC is filed on a separate tax return, unlike a single-member LLC or sole proprietor. The form used to file profit and losses from a multi-member LLC is Form 1065. The entity itself does not pay taxes even though it's on a separate tax return. That's just for reporting and filing purposes.

Please see the illustration of Form 1065 below.

Notice the title "U.S. Return of Partnership Income." Multi-member LLCs are also reported on this form because the tax code treats them as partnerships.

Again, this entity does not pay tax. It's just reporting income and expenses and subsequent profits or losses as a result. The actual profits or losses are allocated to the members based on their operating agreement in the form of a K-1. Each member must report their K-1 on their individual tax return. Please see the illustration below.

Each member will receive this form when the partnership return is filed. This is not done manually. We use software. As a result of inputting the information in the software for a multi-member LLC, a K-1 is automatically produced. Subsequently, each partner should receive their K-1 for their own tax return. This is easily demonstrated in "Tax Strategies Mastermind" when we use visuals and software to teach.

Important Rules: Because multi-member LLCs are treated as partnerships for tax purposes, it's important to note the responsibilities that come along with them.

The Tax Equity and Fiscal Responsibility Act (TEFRA) has governed the procedures for auditing partnerships since 1982. Under TEFRA, if the IRS audited a partnership, any federal income tax liabilities remained with the applicable partners rather than the partnership. Under the old audit rules, the IRS would apply any audit changes to the existing partners, and in turn, the partners would amend their tax returns to reflect these changes.

The old audit rules required partnerships to designate one partner as the Tax Matters Partner. The Tax Matters Partner was the only party permitted to act as a liaison between the IRS and the partners and had limited power to bind partners to the final resolution of an audit.

Under the new rules, there's no longer a Tax Matters Partner. They are called "partnership representatives," and they have sole authority to act on behalf of the partnership. All partners are bound by the actions of the partnership representative, and partners have no statutory right to receive notice of or to participate in the partnership-level proceedings.

The new rules provide for the assessment and collection of tax deficiencies at the partnership level: The IRS can now target the partnership itself to collect a tax deficiency.

What does this mean? When you form a multi-member LLC, you must designate a partnership representative to be the representative in any audit for the LLC. This person can accept or reject any change that is made by the examiner. They do not have to confer with the other members, and those members are bound to any result agreed upon by the designated partnership representative.

The partnership representative is to be designated by the members of the partnership on its annual tax return. The partnership representative may be a partner of the partnership but is not required to. The partnership representative must have a substantial presence in the United States, have a U.S. address, and a U.S. tax ID number.

In other words, be careful to designate a trusted person as your partnership representative for your multi-member LLC.

I want to stress that multi-member LLCs, for tax purposes, are treated as partnerships. They adhere to the requirements of partnerships for tax purposes.

How is this important? Partners get taxed on their *allocated* share of the partnership's profit, even if nothing was distributed to them.

Example: Mark, Janet, and Thomas are partners in a small ice cream shop. Based on their operating agreement, they will split all profits and losses evenly.

The ice cream shop made $60,000 in profits. Each is entitled to $20,000. They collectively decide not to distribute the funds to each of them but to reinvest it into the ice cream shop. Each of them will still get a K-1 for their portion ($20,000 each) and must report it as income on their individual tax return, even though they did not distribute it. It is still considered income for the year to each of them.

S CORPORATIONS

S corporations aren't formed; they are designated, as it is a tax designation. LLCs are a business designation. You must first form your LLC with your secretary of state, then designate S corporation status via the IRS with Form 2553.

The requirements for S corporations are as follows:
- Be a domestic corporation
- Have only allowable shareholders
    - May be individuals, certain trusts, and estates
    - May not be partnerships, corporations, or non-resident alien shareholders
- Have no more than 100 shareholders
- Have only one class of stock

- Not be an ineligible corporation (i.e., certain financial institutions, insurance companies, and domestic international sales corporations)

For most small business owners, you don't have to worry about the class of stock. I'm simply noting it for technical purposes. Most individuals also do not have to worry about having more than 100 shareholders. We do have to note that instead of being called members, as in LLCs, the owners are called shareholders.

An S corporation, like the others, is a pass-through entity. It operates much like an LLC. S corporations report profits and losses on Form 1120-S. The shareholders or owners also receive a K-1 for their share of profit or losses to be reported on their respective individual income tax returns, just like with multi-member LLCs.

A single-member LLC or a multi-member LLC can designate S corporation status. An S corporation may have from one owner (shareholder) up to 100. Many small business owners are single-shareholder S corporations (one owner) or two-shareholder S corporations (married couples). You can, however, have more.

When should you transition to an S corporation?

In short, when your business makes enough income to pay the owners a reasonable salary. We discussed this in the prior chapter, as well as how to research what is reasonable based on your industry and sales.

It's mandated that an S corporation pays the owners because an S-corp doesn't pay self-employment tax. Many people are advised to designate an S-corp without knowing and understanding that you still have to pay yourself a reasonable salary. When you pay yourself a salary, you have to pay employer taxes like Social Security and Medicare, so you still have to end up paying some form of taxes. The only difference is that employer taxes are tax-deductible. So, it *does* benefit you in a lot of ways to designate an S-corp. You just have to pay yourself a reasonable salary. What will happen in an audit is the examiner may revoke your S-corp status. What does that mean? If they take away your S-corp status, you will go back to being an LLC, whether a multi-member or a single-member LLC, and you'll have to pay back self-employment tax. And then you can't designate S-corp status for five years following the year after it was revoked. And so we want to make sure that we designate S-corp when we can afford to pay ourselves a salary.

I want to point out that paying yourself a salary is not transferring money from your business bank account to your personal bank account. That's called an "owner's draw" and is completely allowable. It is not payroll because you do not have taxes withheld from your pay, and you are not remitting employer taxes as required.

C CORPORATION

A C-corp is the only entity that actually pays taxes on its own return. It is not informational. It is reported on a regular Form 1120, and the profits and losses are taxed at the entity level on that tax return. It also does not pay self-employment tax, but unlike an S-corp, a multi-member LLC, a single-member LLC, or a sole proprietor, a C-corp has what you call double taxation. What's double taxation? Because a C-corp is its own entity and pays its own taxes, it is not a pass-through like the other entities. You will pay tax at the entity level. And you also, as an owner or an officer, have to pay yourself a salary. Now, you have to pay taxes on your salary and any dividends. So, the pitfall of a C-corp is double taxation. Now, when do you utilize a C-corp? When you have a large project, and it usually requires maybe up to a thousand or so investors. Maybe you want to get more investors. You want to engage in public funds and issue stock. That's when you would do a C-corp—when you have extremely large profits.

Now that we have identified the different types of business structures and how they translate to the tax return, let's take a look at how to utilize these structures and the different strategies that can be applied.

CHAPTER 5

Business Ownership & Strategy

BUSINESS OWNERSHIP

As we saw in the previous chapter, businesses are allowed to deduct ordinary and necessary expenses under Section 162, unlike individuals who rely on their W-2 income. As a W-2 earner, you cannot deduct any day-to-day expenses. When I recommend that you move within the tax code and shift your income from personal to business (which is ordinary income to extraordinary income—business activities including real estate), I mean to highlight that businesses, which are essentially the wealthy, pay the least amount of income taxes, as discussed earlier.

Before we get into strategy, we have to revisit a very important part of business ownership: actually being defined as a business. Section 162 of the tax code states, "There shall be allowed as a deduction all the ordinary and necessary expenses paid or incurred during the taxable year in carrying on any *trade or business*."

The IRS does not allow hobby expenses. So, what are the components of solidifying yourself as a business?

"A trade or business is generally an activity carried on for livelihood or in good faith to *make a profit*. The facts and circumstances of each case determine whether or not an activity is a trade or business.

The *regularity* of activities and transactions and the *production of income* are important elements. You do not need to actually make a profit to be in a trade or business as long as you have a profit motive. You do need, however, to make ongoing efforts to further the interests of your business."

This comes straight from the IRS. Key items are your intent to make a profit and the regularity of activities and transactions to produce income. Hobbies are more recreational activities that are not intended to generate a profit. You can have income from a hobby without intending to make a profit.

So, what are some activities that define a business?

Material Participation

The time and effort you put into the activity that indicates you intend to make it profitable is called material participation. Within the IRS code, material participation is *over* 500 hours involved in business activity a year (501 or more). That equates to about 1.5 hours a day dedicated to your business. This can easily be identified by your recordkeeping activities. Someone with one small transaction every two months will not be deemed a business. If those transactions are large amounts due to, say, a contract, then you may be considered a business.

Trademarking

Nothing says "this is a business," like trademarking your name.

A trademark can be any word, phrase, symbol, design, or combination of these things that identifies your goods or services. It's how consumers recognize your brand and distinguish your business from competitors.

Your first step is doing a search on the United States Patent and Trademark Office (USPTO) website for your business name. This is completely free. You can do a basic word search for your business name, and if it's available, contact an attorney and have them start the process for you. You can do it yourself, but there are complexities to the process, like choosing the right class for your business products or services. This costs money per class of item. Your business may have multiple goods and services under your brand and because of this, you will need to select the class of items for your trademark. Let an attorney do the work. The

USPTO has examiners who may request additional information that is best handled by an attorney. If you, as the business owner, don't do things correctly, the time may lapse for your trademark and you will have to start the process all over again.

Formation

We went through the different types of business structures in the previous chapter. Now, you need to decide what is best for your business, depending on where you are in the process. Under many circumstances, you should wait until you are out of the start-up phase before you actually incorporate (LLC). This is because you may not be entirely sure about moving forward. As humans, we are fallible and may change our minds, become disinterested, not have enough funds, or have outside circumstances that prevent us from finding the time and making an effort to qualify the activities as a business.

Once you are sure about your business and have dedicated time and energy into the start-up phase, as you exit the start-up phase, for most small business owners, this is when you should form your LLC. Most states allow online formation through the respective state's Secretary of State website. Many times, the online process is instantaneous. You will get your Articles of Organization and Operating Agreement after answering questions and filling out the requested information. These items are usually sent to the email you designate. I suggest a business email (Support@businessname.com). This can usually be done through your selected web hosting provider.

Simultaneously, when forming your business structure with the secretary of state, you need an Employer Identification Number (EIN). This is completely free on the IRS website. Simply visit www.irs.gov and type *"EIN"* in the search bar. Then select "Apply for an Employer Identification Number (EIN) Online." You will be prompted to apply online and taken through the process with the EIN assistant. It's a simple and easy process in which you will answer the sequence of questions as it relates to your business. Most likely, you will choose a limited liability company (LLC) as the structure. Then, you will choose the number of members and the state in which your business operates. There is a tutorial in "Tax Strategies Mastermind," as visual aids are more effective. This process is no longer than 15 minutes, and you will get your EIN immediately. This is located on Form SS-4 from the IRS, which has been emailed to you. Again, I suggest you use an email set up for your business, but it's no big deal to use a personal email.

Recordkeeping

You must carry on the activity in a business-like manner: Maintain a complete and accurate set of books and records. Remember Section 6001? You must have solid financial records, including your recordkeeping.

After you have formed your LLC, you should take your Articles of Organization, Form SS-4, a piece of identification (i.e., driver's license), and a piece of official correspondence with your name and address on it and head straight to a bank and open a business bank account. This is a must for solidifying yourself as a business and not a hobby. I suggest using a bank with an actual branch where you can have a business banking relationship manager. It's always better to have someone in person to talk to for your business banking needs.

In the process, you should apply for a business credit card. Hopefully, your personal credit is decent enough because it's usually necessary for your new business to obtain a credit card, as you are the guarantor.

> **Pro tip:** You will want a Visa or Mastercard for your business credit card, as American Express does not report *positive* items on your credit report for your business. These items are on-time payments and balances. American Express only reports *negative* items, such as late payments. This is important for building business credit.

Business Credit

Once you have your business bank account and credit card, you want to obtain a **DUNS number** from Dun & Bradstreet. What is a DUNS number? "The Dun & Bradstreet D-U-N-S® Number is a unique nine-digit identifier for businesses that is associated with a business's Live Business Identity, which may help evaluate potential partners, seek new contracts, apply for loans, and so much more." You can visit www.dnb.com and apply online. You will be assigned someone to walk you through the functionality of your new Dun & Bradstreet online capabilities. This is also an activity that says, "I'm a business."

STRATEGY

So now that we have solidified your activities as business activities and not a hobby, let's talk about strategy.

Retirement

Business owners can set up a retirement plan under which they can contribute up to three times more than their employee counterparts. For 2024, they can contribute up to $69,000. Imagine the compounding interest on your retirement account at this amount each year. This amount also increases every year. This is why *Forbes* calls it the "$100 Million Dollar 401(k)."

Hiring Family

They can transfer wealth to their family by hiring their children and other family members. Look at your local Chinese restaurant. Likely, it is family-owned and operated. Your local Italian restaurant is also family-owned and operated. The laundromat. The list goes on. In my years as an IRS Examiner, I can't tell you how many times I've seen the same last names on Form 1125-E, Compensation of Officers. In my years of starting my own business, I've found an unbelievable number of individuals who assumed this would be illegal. Clearly, they haven't scanned the IRS website, which has a whole page dedicated to this subject. I'm here to open your eyes. At a very young age, your child can start to build wealth exponentially. All of this is tax-deductible to your business and funds your child's financial success. Knowing your child is financially set up for success is a relief to most parents.

Control

They can significantly control their tax liability by utilizing expenses and tracking in real time. You can't deduct any expenses on your personal return, so you must do it through your business. Every year, my students and I track our tax liability in real time so we can utilize business expenses to reduce our tax liability. Remember, they must be ordinary and necessary, but they do not need to be indispensable. I can spend $5,000 in advertising or $50,000 in advertising, each of which can be justifiable business operations. Advertising is a legitimate expense. It proves intent to profit. Perhaps you want to expand your business, and therefore, your expenses may also expand. This is completely normal in business.

Perhaps you hire your adult child to help you with visits because your client base is growing. You may need an additional vehicle dedicated to business in order to keep up with demand otherwise you may lose business due to failure to meet the growing need. Your additional vehicle can be deductible under Section 179 and Bonus Depreciation (refer to Chapter 3 for further details on this).

Phantom Expenses

This is probably the most important strategy in business ownership: Expenses you don't actually pay but which are "gifted" by the IRS tax code. Depreciation is the number one single reason wealth is accumulated. Imagine making profits in your business but not paying tax on those profits because the tax code does not recognize those profits due to depreciation expenses (phantom expense). That extra vehicle you need for your business can have bonus depreciation in addition to Section 179. That's an additional allocated expense for your vehicle in the year you purchase and use it that you don't pay, which can offset your tax liability greatly.

Depreciation is a huge strategy in real estate as well. Again, I dedicated a whole separate chapter to real estate so you can see the power of depreciation.

Qualified Business Income Deduction (QBI)

QBI is defined as net business income from pass-through entities, excluding income generated outside the United States.

In other words, if your *total* taxable income (not just your business income) is at or below yearly limits, you may qualify for the 20% deduction on your taxable business income. This is best seen in planning throughout the year.

So, let's talk about the difference between the individual return versus the business return. The business return is set up so that you have your income minus your expenses. Then, whatever is left over is what's taxed. This gives the business owner the opportunity to pay lower taxes by pumping more money into their expenses. You have a chance to spend that money on your business instead of paying tax. If you knew you were going to owe the IRS $10,000 in taxes, would you rather pump that money into your advertising, your new computer, new equipment, paying your children, your vehicle, or your marketing team, or would you rather leave it and cut a check to Uncle Sam? This is why I teach my students in Mastermind to track their tax liability in real time using the software in our books and records. Not only that, you also have a lot more benefits on the business tax return. You can pay yourself a salary if you're set up in the right way. You can pay your kids a salary. You can contribute to a business retirement plan that is three times more than your employer-sponsored plan, and every year, the benefit of being in business goes up. We'll go into your retirement planning and the significant difference later on.

But there's a tremendous opportunity via the structure of the return to not pay taxes by paying the money into your expenses first because that's what the business tax return allows. It allows you to pay your expenses first, and then you tax what's left over. And this is the government's way of saying, "Hey, if you don't do it, we're going to take it."

Now, let's get into the personal side. You have your wages minus your taxable income on those wages. Then you get to pay your bills. See, with businesses, they get to pay their bills first. You have no receipt relief on the personal tax return. You can contribute to your traditional retirement, which most people in America cannot max out because of pressing needs like housing, food, daycare, utilities, transportation expenses, and the like. The other items that you can tackle are your medical expenses. And that's only for expenses that exceed 7.5% of your adjusted gross income. Most people cannot pay out of pocket excess of 7.5% of their adjusted gross income in medical and dental expenses. And then there's your primary residence, which I will explain in further detail. Since the Tax Cuts and Jobs Act, your primary residence provides no more benefit on the tax return than it does for a renter. And again, I'll go into detail with the key differences later on in this book.

If you use it right, as we'll discuss in the next chapters, this bonus depreciation can result in over $100,000 in expenses many times, depending on your property's purchase price. It's an expense allocated to the items that are not part of the structure. So you get your regular depreciation, and then you get depreciation for any items that have a useful life under 20 years—things like your appliances, your kitchen cabinets, countertops, flooring, etc. (Your roof doesn't count.) Do you have to do any renovations? No, you just get it. It's an allocated expense, just like depreciation is an allocated expense.

It's not an expense you actually have to pay for. Imagine being able to expense items you already paid for when purchasing the property without doing any renovations. You're allowed to expense these items in the first year the property is available for rent. Understanding the tax code can help you see the impact of this significant expense. Don't worry about the terminology; I'll simplify it for you. It's just tax code terminology, but I want you to understand the difference between personal and business investments, particularly as a real estate investor, and how the tax code views each.

You can see that for a primary residence, the tax code can damage the owner's net worth, while benefiting investors. The tax code expanded an expense typically reserved for new builders, extending it to the average investor. Over the last five years (2019-2024), I've increased my net worth to multi-millions through real estate and business ownership, as the tax code favors business ownership. Much of this was through real estate, which can also offset business profits if done correctly.

I'll show you exactly how this works in future chapters.

COMMON MYTHS

Filing a Tax Return is Voluntary

This is not true. The word "voluntary" refers to the system of allowing taxpayers, on their own (voluntarily), to determine the correct amount of tax and complete the appropriate returns rather than have the government determine tax for them. The requirement to file an income tax return is stated in Internal Revenue Code §§ 6011(a), 6012(a), et seq., and 6072(a).

The Supreme Court's opinion in *Flora v. United States,* 362 U.S. 145, 176 (1960), is often referenced for the position that "our system of taxation is based upon voluntary assessment and payment, not upon distraint."

Case Law for Reference:
Helvering v. Mitchell
United States v. Tedder
United States v. Richards
Woods v. Commissioner
Johnson v. Commissioner

Paying Tax is Voluntary, as Filing a Tax Return is Voluntary

IRC Section 1 of the Internal Revenue Code imposes a tax on the taxable income of individuals, estates, and trusts as determined by the tables set forth in that section. (Section 11 imposes a tax on the taxable income of corporations.) Furthermore, the obligation to pay tax is described in IRC Section 6151, which requires taxpayers to submit payment with their tax returns. Failure to pay taxes could subject the non-complying individual to criminal penalties, including fines and imprisonment, as well as civil penalties.

Case Law for Reference:
United States v. Bressler
Schiff v. United States
Packard v. United States
United States v. Gerads

In short, you are required to file a tax return, or the government will do it for you, and you are required to pay any and all amounts owed.

Being a Structure Versus Being in Business

We talked about actually forming the structure, but there's a difference between structure and actual operations being in business. The IRS sees substance over form—what you're actually doing versus what you look like you're doing.

Example: People open an LLC thinking that they can purchase a business vehicle because they have an LLC, because in their minds, an LLC is automatically a business, but you have no operations. So the vehicle that you purchase can't really be considered for business purposes because you don't have any operations. The tax benefits don't come from being an LLC. They come from actual operations. So a lot of people think they can take these everyday expenses because, well, they have an LLC. You only have an entity structure. *You do not have an actual business without operations.*

PREMATURE FORMATION

Many people want to start a business, but it's often not well planned out, and they don't know where to begin. They think, *Hey, I need to start an LLC*, which is relatively easy to form online in many states, typically taking less than 30 minutes to establish your LLC and get your Articles of Organization. Most businesses start with an LLC because it separates you from the business legally, though, for tax purposes, an LLC is just a business designation, not a separate entity. This leads to the misconception that forming an LLC automatically makes you a business, which is far from the truth.

We'll discuss business structures in this book, but to give a quick overview: You have a sole proprietorship where you and the business are not separated legally—an LLC, which can be single-member or multi-member; and an S-corp, a tax designation that requires forming an LLC first.

A single-member LLC is treated as a sole proprietorship for tax purposes, while a multi-member LLC is treated as a partnership, filing a Form 1065.

Many people go *LLC crazy*, thinking forming an LLC is the be-all and end-all. They start with a business idea, are automatically a Schedule C, and then solidify their business by forming an LLC, separating themselves legally from the entity. However, forming an LLC doesn't automatically make it a business; it just establishes the entity under which it operates.

Operations make a business an actual business activity. For example, some people form an LLC with no operations, income, or expenses. The IRS sees a Schedule C sole proprietor as a business due to its operations, but an LLC with no operations isn't recognized as a business. **Operations** mean consistent income and expenses. You have the intent to profit and you have a designated business bank account. You have proper recordkeeping and documentation. You have a business credit card.

It's important to solidify your business as separate from you personally, but even more important is to ensure you have actual operations. Just forming an LLC online doesn't make you a business; it merely establishes an entity, which is the structure under which you're conducting business. Many people think having an LLC automatically qualifies them for loans, but lending isn't guaranteed simply because you have a business entity. You need to show actual finances, just as you would for a personal loan or mortgage. Without operations, the LLC is just a structure, not a business. Many LLC owners don't engage in business activities as defined by the Internal Revenue Code: an intent to make a profit through consistent and frequent involvement. You must have what's called material participation in your business operations. Material participation, as discussed earlier in this chapter regarding short-term rentals, means being actively engaged in business activities for *over* 500 hours a year (501 hours or more), demonstrating an intent to make a profit.

Another mistake many small business owners make, particularly early on, is not filing a tax return because they think, "Well, I didn't really make much money." Even if you have a loss, you need to file a return. Not filing when you have income is tax evasion. In fact, losses can be beneficial, especially for business owners with a W-2 job. Your job income likely fuels your business activities, and filing losses with material participation can offset your W-2 income from your job. Ensure you have material participation to avoid being considered a hobby—open a business bank account and form an LLC if you're truly invested. Then, file those losses to take full advantage of your business activities. And so what ends up happening is all those withholdings that are coming from your job income are being earned back into your bank account by spending it in your business.

As discussed previously, I discourage people from forming an LLC prematurely. Many things can happen in this process. I suggest starting as a sole proprietor, meaning not forming anything during the start-up phase. People often lose interest, or the original partners may drop out. For example, you might discuss starting a mobile pet grooming company at Thanksgiving, but after the holidays, others decide not to invest in materials, supplies, or a van, leaving you without funding. This results in an LLC that's no longer used. This is problematic, as it comes with administrative obligations, including filing state tax returns. Failing to do so incurs penalties. For federal purposes, it's a bit different. If you designate S-corp status, you must pay yourself a reasonable salary, file both federal and state returns, and face penalties if you don't. Additionally, you have to consider state filing fees, which can be annual or biannual. The Corporate Transparency Act now mandates business owners to file an informational report with their secretary of state, showing who owns the LLC and associated information. Failure to file can result in daily penalties. Thus, it's best not to form an LLC until you're ready. My advice is to keep your start-up costs separate on a personal credit card until you know your business will start, everyone is interested and invested, and you're ready to go. At that point, you can form your LLC, which will have operations and commit to an administrative structure.

And again, you must have operations. Without them, you're not a business—just a structure. I stress the importance of actual business activities because deductions are the easy part; the foundation is not. The most important part of your activities is setting up a solid foundation: Establish your structure, have an appropriate bank account for your business, and a business credit card to separate business activities from personal ones. You also need material participation, which must be frequent, concurrent, and driven by an intent to make a profit.

For example, if you're a W-2 employee and most of your living expenses are paid from your job, and you don't generate much income from the business you started on the side (not a side hustle, but a business you started on the side), and you don't show an appropriate bank account, records, expenses, or involvement, the IRS may consider it a hobby. Conversely, if you're generating substantial income, have invested in advertising and equipment, and have the proper structure, it's difficult for the IRS to deem it a hobby.

So, in any business, whether in start-up or seasoned phase, ensure you're solidified. Consider trademarking, for instance. Trademarking your name and logo signifies you're serious about your business—something hobbyists don't typically do. I'll provide a list on the next page of things that define your business as an actual business, not a hobby.

CHAPTER 6

Real Estate Investment and Strategy

In this chapter we'll explore the difference between real estate as a personal versus an investment property. The Tax Cuts and Jobs Act of 2017 marked a turning point, as any changes in the tax code typically favor business over personal activities.

Some people argue that they have appreciation on their primary residence, but appreciation is phantom—it isn't realized until recognized, meaning it can't be counted until it's in your account. Just ask the homeowners from 2008 during the housing crash. Many went underwater, lost their jobs, and couldn't pay their mortgages, leading to foreclosures and turning them into renters.

As of 2017, the standard deduction has increased and will continue to do so, while mortgage interest decreases as more is paid into the principal. This means your standard deduction will often outweigh itemized deductions, including mortgage interest and property taxes, offering no more benefit than renting. This situation is likely to persist unless there's a significant tax code change.

The government is essentially saying, "We don't care about your personal activities. We don't care that you purchased a home or that it's your primary residence. We're giving you nothing." In fact, recent tax law changes have taken away benefits.

Real estate has been the reason for the most exponential growth in net worth.

The goal is to make you aware of the tax implications of owning real estate through the eyes of an investor versus through the eyes of a homeowner and how building wealth with real estate starts with being an investor. There are four main elements of utilizing investment properties:

- Depreciation
- Bonus depreciation
- Real estate professional status (long-term rentals)
- Short-term rental loophole (short-term rentals)

Depreciation and bonus depreciation create phantom expenses. The last item tells the tax code that real estate losses created by depreciation and bonus depreciation can offset all other income, not just rental (passive income), because now the investment activity is "active." Let's go through each item.

DEPRECIATION

Depreciation assumes that the rental property is actually declining over time as a result of wear and tear. We know this is not necessarily true, but as per the tax code, this is how all assets used in business are treated.

We need to know the useful life of the property in order to calculate depreciation. Again, in "Tax Strategies Mastermind," we use over-the-counter tax software to do the calculations for us. There's no need for pen and paper. In fact, I would never recommend trying to calculate anything; just let the software do the work. But for illustrative purposes, let's walk through the depreciation expense. For properties with four units or under that are rentals, including single-families that are rentals, the useful life is 27.5 years. The purchase price minus land value equals your depreciable basis for your property. Let's do the math.

Let's say you purchase a multifamily for $700,000. You look up the land value of your property on your county tax assessor or clerk's website. I like to do a Google search: "find my land value city, state" or "find my land value, county name." You will likely be led to the county's site for property records. From there, you can do some digging. Or I like to use PropertyShark.com. You have to pay for a membership after the first free search. Again, I show this in visual aid in Mastermind. Now that you've looked up your land value and found that it was, say, $50,000, you will subtract that from your purchase price. This will leave you with what is your depreciable basis for the property, $650,000. This amount will be divided by the useful life. In this case, we will assume it's four units and under, so $650,000 divided by 27.5 years. This leaves you with a yearly depreciation expense of $23,636 that you are allotted. This is an expense that reduces your income that you don't actually pay. See the illustration below.

Purchase Price $700K
-Land Value $50K
Depreciable Basis $650K ÷ **27.5 Years**

Depreciation $23,636 Per Year

BONUS DEPRECIATION

This item was granted to real estate investors as a result of the 2017 Tax Cuts & Jobs Act (TCJA). It is simply what it states: bonus depreciation or additional expense. You also don't pay this expense. It is phantom, just like regular depreciation. You can only take bonus depreciation in the first year the property is **placed in service**, meaning it's ready and available for rent. You may not have an actual renter in place, but it's ready to go. Say you purchased a ready-to-go property on 12/20/2022. Whether you have renters in place from the previous owner or you need to find your own renters, if it's ready for rent, it's placed in service for 2022. Therefore, you would take bonus depreciation for the tax year 2022.

What is bonus depreciation? It is the process of identifying personal property assets that are grouped with real property assets and separating out personal assets for tax reporting purposes. Sounds confusing, right? In layman's terms, you get regular depreciation for your property as calculated above. Then, for the first year you rent it, you get an additional expense for items that have a useful life of under 20 years. Bonus depreciation is separated by items that have a 5-year useful life and a 15-year useful life. Things like appliances, kitchen countertops, removable flooring, carpeting, and ceiling fans are considered 5-year items. Fencing, driveway, and other site improvements have a 15-year useful life. Your roof is not included in any bonus depreciation. Let's look at the illustration below.

The first item is your actual real property, the structure itself. You get regular depreciation every year for it. The second two images are your 5-year and 15-year properties, your appliances and the like, and your fencing and site improvements.

How is bonus depreciation calculated for the 5-year and 15-year properties? You need a **cost segregation study**. This is a report that allocates a specific amount to these items that you can expense in the first year. Remember, the amount of depreciation you get is based on your property's depreciable basis (purchase price minus land value). You must work with a cost segregation study firm. They will ask you for all important documents from the purchase of your property. Once you receive the report, you will have the amounts to expense in the first year.

A common question I get is, "Do I have to have receipts for renovation?" The answer is no because actual property improvement expenses are not deductible. A cost segregation study is the only way to capture a large expense like renovation. In other words, if you *choose* to renovate your property in the first year, you will still have to use the numbers from a cost segregation study. Whether the renovations come out to be more or less, you cannot deviate from the numbers in the study. You do not have to do renovations to get the expense. You are "gifted" this expense for being an investor. I purchased almost all my properties without having to actually renovate them. I was still allowed bonus depreciation as an additional expense as long as they were ready and available for rent. I did, however, purchase one property that was already rented. I had a cost segregation study done as I did for my other properties, except I did renovations on each unit as the current tenants moved out. I could not use the actual expenses for the renovation. I simply just used the cost segregation study for the amounts allocated to my 5-year and 15-year properties to capture the cost. In some cases, if you do renovate, the cost segregation study may capture the actual cost of renovations if you *choose* to do them, and sometimes the actual renovation costs may be higher. You cannot take amounts in excess of the cost segregation study. Remember, you don't have to do renovations to be eligible for bonus depreciation.

What does a cost segregation study look like? You will have the 5-year and 15-year properties separated out with an amount you can expense with each. Please see the illustration below.

Cost Segregation Result Schedule

Building System	Category Description	Allocated Purchase Cost	Life YR	Method	Asset Class
Building Structure and Interiors	Bathroom Vanities	$5,839	27.5	SL	RealProperty
	Roof Structure	$22,977	27.5	SL	RealProperty
	Building Shell & Foundation	$252,256	27.5	SL	RealProperty
	Windows	$11,943	27.5	SL	RealProperty
	Roof Covering	$13,733	27.5	SL	RealProperty
	Other Flooring	$9,403	27.5	SL	RealProperty
	Interior Partitions & Ceilings	$88,900	27.5	SL	RealProperty
	Doors	$11,031	27.5	SL	RealProperty
Plumbing	Bathroom Plumbing & Fixtures	$29,858	27.5	SL	RealProperty
	Water & Waste Utility Services	$2,961	27.5	SL	RealProperty
Building Electrical	Electrical Service & Wiring	$30,905	27.5	SL	RealProperty
	Electrical Utility Services	$1,781	27.5	SL	RealProperty
	Lighting	$14,617	27.5	SL	RealProperty
Fire Protection	Fire Alarms & Devices	$1,850	27.5	SL	RealProperty
Real Property Subtotal		$498,054			

Other Non-Structural Interiors	Appliance Wiring		$2,466	5	200%DB
	Appliances		$12,776	5	200%DB
	Blinds & Curtains		$1,327	5	200%DB
	Carpet		$14,225	5	200%DB
	Ceiling Fans & Wiring		$746	5	200%DB
	Kitchen Cabinets & Countertops		$14,597	5	200%DB
	Kitchen & Appliance Plumbing		$5,106	5	200%DB
	Removable Flooring		$32,685	5	200%DB
Non-Structural Interiors Subtotal			$83,928		
Sitework	Deck/Patio		$18,832	15	150%DB
	Driveway & Walks		$14,495	15	150%DB
	Landscaping		$631	15	150%DB
	Other Site Improvements		$1,559	15	150%DB
Site Work Subtotal			$35,518		
GRAND TOTAL			$617,500		

Above is an example of a bonus depreciation study. I have outlined the 5-year and 15-year items and the associated cost allocated. Again, this is done by a cost segregation study firm or accountant. You will not do this manually or calculate this on your own. You must pay for the report. It is tax-deductible. We work with a cost segregation provider in "Tax Strategies Mastermind."

Example: Using the same example as above, where the purchase price minus the land value (depreciable basis) of the rental property is $650,000, the annual depreciation expense calculated was $23,636 (refer to the previous example if need be). Now we get to add bonus depreciation based on the cost segregation study example.

BONUS DEPRECIATION EXAMPLE

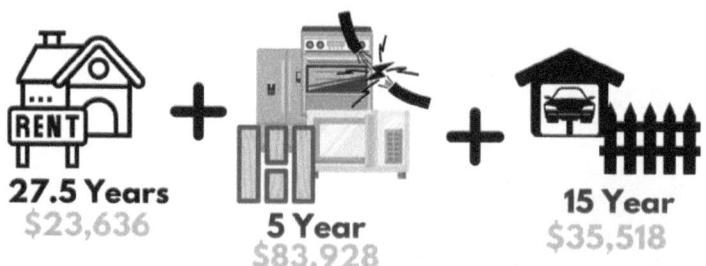

27.5 Years $23,636 + **5 Year** $83,928 + **15 Year** $35,518

Total FOR YEAR 1 $143,082

In this example, we are allowed the regular depreciation (which is every year) plus the bonus depreciation, which comes from the cost segregation study in our above illustration, for a total depreciation in year one of $143,082. This is a large expense you, as a real estate investor, are "gifted" for engaging in rental activities. You do not get bonus depreciation in any other years. If you find yourself eligible for bonus depreciation under the Tax Cuts & Jobs Act, but you never took advantage of it, you can recapture it on your current return with what's called a change of accounting (Form 3115). Your accountant or cost segregation study firm can provide this.

Eligibility

Under The Tax Cuts and Jobs Act, properties purchased and placed in service (rental) between September 27, 2017, and December 31, 2026, are eligible for bonus depreciation.

If you purchased a property in 2005, for example, your property is not eligible for bonus depreciation under the Tax Cuts & Jobs Act.

If you purchased a property in 2018 and made it a primary residence, then converted it to a rental in, say, 2020, you may be eligible for bonus depreciation.

Bonus depreciation has a schedule; I will lay it out and explain what it means. As per the Tax Cuts and Jobs Act, the bonus depreciation schedule was as follows:

- 100% for property placed in service 9/17/2017–12/31/2022
- 80% for property placed in service 2023
- 60% for property placed in service 2024
- 40% for property placed in service 2025
- 20% for property placed in service 2026

Under the 47th administration, the schedule of Bonus Depreciation has been edited due to the passage of The One Big Beautiful Bill, which reinstituted 100% bonus depreciation for property placed in service for 2025 moving forward. The phaseout prior to the passage of the bill is no longer valid.

So what do these percentages mean? Remember the cost segregation study, which allocates that cost to 5-year and 15-year items that give you the bonus depreciation expense? Depending on when your property was ready and available for rent, that's the percentage of the cost you can take as a bonus depreciation expense. So if you purchased property in, say, 2023, you will get 80% of the numbers allocated to 5-year and 15-year items.

There are certain criteria that need to be met for a property to be eligible for bonus depreciation. There is a Frequently Asked Questions webpage on the IRS website, but I will break down some simple rules here. I encourage you to visit the FAQ page at https://www.irs.gov/newsroom/additional-first-year-depreciation-deduction-bonus-faq.

- The property was not used by the taxpayer or a predecessor at any time prior to such acquisition. An example may be a rent-to-own situation. You used the property prior to purchasing it.
- The property was not acquired from a related party. Who is a related party? Parents, grandparents, kids, grandkids, and siblings. Be careful with in-laws, as someone is related through marriage.
- Inherited property—sorry, but this one may hurt a bit.

Avoiding Capital Gains and Depreciation Recapture

If you sell your investment property, you will have to pay back all the depreciation and bonus depreciation that you took as a rental. This is called depreciation recapture. The IRS is simply saying, "We gave you this phantom expense, you sold it, and now we want it back."

You will also have to pay capital gains tax. This is a tax on the amount of money you made in the sale above what you purchased the property for.

The only way to avoid both is through a 1031 Exchange. This is when you sell a property and use the proceeds to purchase a like-kind property of equal or greater value. Simply put, you are selling the old to upgrade to the new. Perhaps you had a single-family rental, and you want to purchase a duplex or quad. All the proceeds from the sale of the original property would be rolled over into an escrow account through a 1031 exchange intermediary, as the money cannot hit your personal account—it becomes taxable if it does so.

You have 45 days to identify the new property and 180 days total to acquire the new property. The funds from the escrow account through the 1031 exchange intermediary will go directly to the purchase of the new property without touching your bank account. This way, there's no taxable event.

When would you sell without doing a 1031 exchange? When the property is dead weight. You cannot cash flow, you cannot find another property worth purchasing for the returns on the investment, *and* you have huge profits from another property sale to offset, or huge profits from a business activity outside of real estate to offset. This is called harvesting your losses: You have so much money to offset during the tax year that you need a loss to counter this huge influx of taxable income. This requires strategy and planning. You will have to track your tax liability in real time. This is how we teach you to strategize in "Tax Strategies Mastermind."

That's why real estate wealth building is a buy-and-hold strategy. If you plan on selling without reinvesting into another rental property of equal or greater value, then it wouldn't benefit you to utilize bonus depreciation. However, you will have to pay back the regular depreciation taken.

REAL ESTATE PROFESSIONAL STATUS: LONG-TERM RENTALS ONLY

This strategy is what makes bonus depreciation work for you. We have created these huge phantom losses because depreciation is not an actual expense; it's a "gifted" expense that is rewarded to investors. Now, what do we do with these losses?

Normally, under IRC Section 469, real estate investing is a passive activity. This means that any rental activities stay separate from other activities on the tax return. Any losses created, usually by depreciation and bonus depreciation, will only offset rental income. However, we have a thing called Real Estate Professional Status (REPS) in the tax code. Real estate professional status essentially says: Now that you have this huge loss created by depreciation and bonus depreciation, you can use this loss to offset not only rental income but also wages from your regular job and any other income. Now, it's no longer a passive activity. It's considered active. This can essentially wipe out many people's tax liability. We will go through some real numbers for illustration purposes, but let's take a look at the requirements to meet REPS under the Internal Revenue Code.

- More than half of the personal services you performed in all trades or businesses during the tax year were performed in real property trades or businesses in which you materially participated.
- You performed more than 750 hours of services during the tax year in rental property trades or businesses in which you materially participated.

Important words here are "more than." You may hear people spout that 750 hours is all you need. No, "more than" 750 hours. More than half (51%) of your time has to be in real estate rental activities. Most importantly, you have to materially participate. Let's dive deeper into these two items.

If you are a full-time W-2 earner, you will not be able to meet the first requirement, and therefore, you won't be able to meet real estate professional status. But don't leave yet: There is a loophole in the next section we will talk about. The implication is that because you are full-time at your main source of income (our 35–40 hour work week, which is normally documented on your pay stub), it's reasonable for the IRS to assume half of your time is spent at your full-time employment.

If you are a part-time employee, it's reasonable to assume that you can, in fact, spend more time in real estate activities because you aren't spending most of your time under your employer.

Married couples

If you have one spouse who works full-time and another who works part-time or does not work, you can circumvent the first requirement as your non-working spouse or part-time spouse can meet the criteria of

51% or more of their time in real estate activities. If you file a joint return, this works well. But this isn't the exception I speak of for full-time W-2 earners. We will get to that shortly.

Now, let's talk about the activities in the hours requirement. Over 750 hours engaged in real estate activities. The activities specifically laid out by the IRS are as follows with regard to real estate investing activities:

- Develops or redevelops it
- Constructs or reconstructs it
- Acquires it
- Converts it
- Rents or leases it
- Operates or manages it
- Brokers it

Does having a real estate license automatically qualify you as a real estate professional within the IRS? No, you must meet the requirements. The misconception is that an agent automatically qualifies when, in fact, a broker automatically qualifies.

Rule 1: Material Participation

Now, let's talk about the actual activities in depth. Of the 750-plus hours, over 500 hours must be material participation activities. The hours must be attributed to your rental activities. Activities that are considered material are those that you are directly involved with during the day-to-day management of your rentals. Examples may include:

- Supervising renovations
- Lawn care
- Snow removal
- Coordinating or performing repairs/contractor supervision
- Gutter cleaning
- Inspections

What is *not* material participation?

Investor Activities

We must be careful not to confuse material participation with investor participation. These are considered more administrative in nature. You cannot treat the work you do in your capacity as an investor in an activity as participation unless you're directly involved in the day-to-day management or operations of the activity. This includes:
- Studying and reviewing financial statements or reports on operations of the activity.
- Preparing or compiling summaries or analyses of the finances or operations of the activity for your own use.
- Monitoring the finances or operations of the activity in a nonmanagerial capacity.

Let's focus on the word "unless." If you are detailed like me, you will think, *Well, if I am involved in day-to-day operations, as per the IRS, I can count these activities as material.* Let me save you the headache of an audit: Don't count it either way. The IRS Examiner may not be inclined to let you include those activities, and I want to save you the distress of going to tax court to fight over that simple word "unless."

Travel Time

Travel time is also not included in material participation. The IRS has, on numerous occasions, disallowed travel as it is not considered an *integral* activity. In fact, if you are a real estate professional, the IRS takes the position that it is commuting hours and, therefore, not included in material participation.

Example: Let's give an example of someone who meets the material participation rule—John owns four properties. He purchased them as fixer-uppers so he can rent them out. He works part-time at the local mechanic shop three days a week, totaling 20 hours per week. The rest of the time, John supervises his rehabs through hired contractors and does some of the work himself. He goes to Home Depot and picks out the floors and kitchen backsplash. He visits a decor shop to pick out the kitchen countertops. He does some work himself, like painting. He spends his time ensuring each unit is ready and available for rent. He also must meet the property inspector to make sure his properties are up to code. He is there while any contractors are at his properties and chooses that time to do any minor work himself. He must log all hours and what he did. He must maintain any contractor agreements, invoices, payments, and correspondence. John has 830 hours in material participation for the year between all his properties, including finding tenants. John meets material participation rules.

Note: John cannot include travel time to and from his properties in his hours or any administrative hours like insurance payments or rent analysis.

Rule 2: Active Participation

Active participation is another test that must be met. Active participation has two facets:
- You make significant management decisions that include approving new tenants, deciding on rental terms, approving expenditures, etc.
- You own at least 10% of the property.

Most of us meet the active participation guidelines unless you hand over all responsibility to a property management company. In that case, you risk losing REPS altogether.

What if you don't meet the material participation requirements but you meet active participation requirements? This is most full-time wage earners. Again, we will discuss a loophole for you to take advantage of the same benefits, but for now, let's assume you only meet active participation, which is common.

Real Estate Loss Allowance For Non-Professionals

- Up to $25,000 may be deducted as a real estate loss per year as long as the individual's adjusted gross income is $100,000 or less.

- The deduction phases out for individuals earning between $100,000 and $150,000. People with higher adjusted gross incomes are not eligible for the deduction.

This is what most people hear from their CPAs or tax preparers, as most full-time earners only meet active participation rules. They don't explain to people that they can actually take all losses if they meet material participation requirements as well.

So let's sum this up, because real estate professional status can be confusing. You must meet the following criteria:

1. Over 50% of your time has to be spent in real estate activities for your rental(s)
   - You cannot be a full-time employee
   - You must spend more time in real estate than any other activity (*over* 50%)
2. You must have *over* 750 hours involved in these real estate activities (751-plus hours)
   - Of the 750 hours, over 500 must be material. The other 250-plus can be general activities, like seminars, networking events, and conferences
   - Travel and investor activities cannot be counted as material participation hours
3. You must own at least 10% of the property and make major management decisions, such as approving tenants.

Pro tip: Try to make *well over* 500 hours of material participation. Do not document the minimum. In an audit, you want to be protected from an examiner disallowing hours. Also, try to go above and beyond 750-plus hours. Lastly, do not pad activities with over-exaggerated hours. It doesn't take an hour to sweep the walkway. An examiner will see right through this and disallow all hours.

SHORT-TERM RENTAL (STR) LOOPHOLE

What about my full-time wage earners? You can't meet the criteria of *over* 50% of your time spent in real estate activities. This is an implication in the tax code not specifically stated, but will be disallowed even if you meet the 750-plus hour rule. This is because it's implied that you spend most of your time during your employer's hours. So how do we get around this? The short-term rental loophole! Let's give you the IRS verbiage first. Your activity isn't a rental activity under IRC Section 469 if any of the following apply (straight from the IRS website):

1. The average period of customer use of the property is 7 days or less. You calculate the average period of customer use by dividing the total number of days in all rental periods by the number of rentals during the tax year. If the activity involves renting more than one class of property, multiply the average period of customer use of each class by a fraction. The numerator of the fraction is the gross rental income from that class of property, and the denominator is the activity's total gross rental income. The activity's average period of customer use will equal the sum of the amounts for each class.

2. The average period of customer use of the property, as calculated in (1) above, is 30 days or less, and you provide significant personal services with the rentals. Significant personal services include only services performed by individuals. To determine if personal services are significant, all relevant facts and circumstances are taken into consideration, including the frequency of the services, the type and amount of labor required to perform the services, and the value of the services relative to the amount charged for the use of the property. Significant personal services don't include the following:
   a. Services needed to permit the lawful use of the property.
   b. Services to repair or improve property that would extend its useful life for a period substantially longer than the average rental.

c. Services that are similar to those commonly provided with long-term rentals of real estate, such as cleaning and maintenance of common areas or routine repairs.
3. You provide extraordinary personal services in making the rental property available for customer use. Services are extraordinary personal services if they're performed by individuals and the customers' use of the property is incidental to their receipt of the services.
4. The rental is incidental to a non-rental activity. The rental of property is incidental to an activity of holding property for investment if the main purpose of holding the property is to realize a gain from its appreciation and the gross rental income from the property is less than 2% of the smaller of the property's unadjusted basis or fair market value. The unadjusted basis of property is its cost, which is not reduced by depreciation or any other basis adjustment. The rental of property is incidental to a trade or business activity if all of the following apply:
   a. You own an interest in the trade or business activity during the year.
   b. The rental property was used mainly in that trade or business activity during the current year or during at least two of the five preceding tax years.
   c. Your gross rental income from the property is less than 2% of the smaller of its unadjusted basis or fair market value. Lodging provided to an employee or the employee's spouse or dependents is incidental to the activity or activities in which the employee performs services if the lodging is furnished for the employer's convenience.
5. You customarily make the rental property available during defined business hours for nonexclusive use by various customers.
6. You provide the property for use in a non-rental activity in your capacity as an owner of an interest in the partnership, S corporation, or joint venture conducting that activity.

Sounds confusing? Let me make it simple. If you are a full-time wage earner and cannot utilize REPS (long-term rentals) to offset your tax liability from wages, you can use the short-term rental loophole, as the short-term rental loophole does not require that over 50% of your time be involved in real estate activities. You now have a non-rental business activity. This means your short-term rental is essentially treated like any other business outside of long-term rentals. You do, however, have to materially participate.

To be considered to materially participate in a short-term rental, an investor must pass *one* of the following tests:

1. He/she spent more than 500 hours during the year on their short-term rental.
2. He/she spent more than 100 hours during the year on their short-term rental *and* more than anyone else (including cleaners, PM, etc.).
3. He/she spent substantially ALL the work on this short-term rental.

The easiest of these tests to fulfill would seem to be the over 100-hour test. As a former examiner, I highly encourage the over 500 rule. Taking the easy route can make you a target in an audit. Remember, your hours must be material.

To revisit, material activities include but are not limited to:
- Supervising renovations
- Lawn care
- Snow removal
- Coordinating or performing repairs/contractor supervision
- Gutter cleaning
- Inspections

If you have a property manager, this is going to be difficult for both long-term and short-term rental strategies. An IRS Examiner will likely make you prove that you spent more time involved in your rentals than the property manager. This is more of a self-managing strategy that has huge benefits.

Putting This All Together

We need to combine depreciation and bonus depreciation with REPS or short-term rental strategy.

We first create the phantom losses in our real estate activities with the phantom expenses depreciation and bonus depreciation. Then we use those losses to offset ordinary income via REPS or STR strategies. Let's continue our earlier example of depreciation and combine it with REPS.

Tax-Deductible Expenses

Mortgage interest	$25,000
Property taxes	$9,000
First-year depreciation expense	$143,082
Total expenses	$177,082
Rental income	$50,000
Profit (Loss)	($127,082)

If you don't know by now, when you have more expenses than income, you have a loss. In this case, the loss is phantom (not real) as bonus depreciation and depreciation are not actual expenses paid. In other words, the actual outcome is a profit of $16,000 in your bank account (assuming no repairs, etc.): rental income of $50,000 minus your expenses actually paid ($25,000 plus $9,000).

However, the tax code sees this differently. Those phantom expenses are acknowledged as real expenses even though you don't actually pay them. So, the IRS sees a *loss* of $127,082, not a profit like your real numbers.

This is what rental real estate is supposed to do in the tax code. Now, what do we do with this loss of $127,082? We meet REPS or utilize the STR strategy, and this loss can offset business and/or wage income.

Let's take this example further. Let's say during the year, you also had a wage or business income of $120,000. Those rental losses will offset this income. Because those losses are greater than your income in this example, there's nothing to tax. Remember, you *have* to make your rental activity "active" instead of a passive activity via REPS.

W-2/1099 Income	$120,000
Rental Losses	$127,082
Taxable income	$0

Your rental losses are greater than your income, and since this is no longer a passive activity, you will offset all your other income. Now, you have no tax liability. In fact, you have a leftover loss of $7,082. This will carry forward to the next year, until it can offset your future income.

Most wage earners have their taxes withheld each pay period during the year. Imagine filing your return with your investment property combining bonus depreciation and REPS or STR strategy and being refunded all your withholdings. Sounds worth it? It is.

Documentation

You must document your hours for each activity and provide proof of each activity. One way is to do it manually with folders and archived emails on your computer and an MS Excel spreadsheet of each activity with the date and time spent on the activity. You must be as descriptive as possible. If you're like me, you love a good app. We use REPStracker in "Tax Strategies Mastermind." You can visit www.repstracker.com and plug in promo code "Moneynista" for a discount. The app allows you to document your activities for both short-term and long-term rentals, upload documentation, and document time spent on each activity. The application keeps track of all hours for each year. It allows you to pull a report of hours per year, and all documents are attached in a link. It is important to attach documentation for each activity: You must provide as much proof as possible of each activity.

Example: Let's go back to our prior example to illustrate this—John owns four properties. He purchased them as fixer-uppers so he can rent them out. He works part-time at the local mechanic shop, three days a week, totaling 20 hours per week. The rest of the time, John supervises his rehabs through hired contractors. He goes to Home Depot and picks out the floors and kitchen backsplash. He visits a decor shop to pick out the kitchen countertops. He spends his time fixing each unit up one by one, and as he rents them, he focuses on the other units. He does some work himself, like painting. He is there while any contractors are at his properties and chooses that time to do any minor work himself. He must log all hours and what he did. He must maintain any contractor agreements, invoices, payments, and correspondence. John has 830 hours in material participation for the year between all his properties, including finding tenants. John is a real estate professional according to IRS standards.

John must document every activity per property. Remember, John cannot include travel time. He must keep or upload any receipts and contractor invoices, and estimates per property per activity he logs. Any documentation, including emails and screenshots of texts, also helps. Keep in mind, you have to ensure you are able to prove you were materially involved in the rental activities.

Things like mowing the lawn may not require documentation outside of logging the time spent, but it must make sense. If you have a large property, it may take hours (think acres). If you have a property with a relatively small yard, you may not be able to justify three hours to mow. Hopefully, this is making sense. Padding hours is not a good strategy.

If John had a short-term rental (think Airbnb), his activities might look more like "Turnover cleaning for March stay. Wash linens, dishes, trash removal, patch and paint holes, steam clean couch, bed bug treatment, replace light bulb." This may justify hours and receipts as proof. You get the gist. John also has the Airbnb app to prove the bookings.

Documentation is the most critical aspect of building wealth in the tax code. It's important you start to think like an auditor.

Bonus Item: Protecting Your Cash Flow

As a bonus, I'm going to give you something not related to tax but which is definitely valuable to securing your income through real estate. I am an auditor. That is the foundation for all my knowledge. This means that, above all, I approach wealth building with preventive measures. One such measure as a real estate investor (a landlord) is to utilize lease protection insurance.

This is completely separate from your homeowner's insurance for rentals. This is a third-party product that ensures you, as the landlord, are compensated should your tenants default on rent. I like to use TheGuarantors. There are several companies that offer such insurance, so you may have to Google other options.

The first step is to register your property. This is free. Your property is now part of a landlord portal, in the case of TheGuarantors. You will simply make sure they cover your city and state for lease protection. When you are ready to rent your unit, simply invite the applicant via email to apply through the landlord portal. In the case of TheGuarantors, they will do the credit and income check on the applicant and require you to input the rent amount for the unit along with the length of the lease and desired months of coverage. Based on the profile of the applying tenant, they will come up with the one-time premium (fee) for the lease. This is payable by the tenant. I like to waive the security deposit, as it may create financial hardship for the tenant. Paying a premium and the first month's rent to move in should suffice. If they are approved, they will be prompted to pay the premium. Once paid, you will get a lease bond that states the coverage, which should be the full length of the lease. That is when you prepare and issue the lease to the tenant and collect the first month's rent.

This process helps ensure the best quality of tenants. A good rule of thumb is that if a tenant only wants a year lease, I still require 24 months of coverage as most tenants renew, and you don't want to bother them with another premium.

If your tenant defaults on your rental payments, you must begin the eviction process. Once the unit is in your possession, you will submit a claim to the insurance company. They will reimburse you for any back rent owed and any rent moving forward until the lease expires or until you rent the unit again.

Each company has a different process, and processes within a single company change periodically, so be sure to keep up with the requirements of whichever company you choose. Also, note that some locations aren't covered for rentals due to the high risk of non-payment. Make sure you check out all options.

Recap

Now that I've given you the blueprint for tax flow and protecting your cash flow, let's drive the bigger picture home. I want to note that the strategies for real estate are all *separate*. You can take bonus depreciation and not meet REPS or STR. They are not required to be paired; however, when combined, you get the optimal outcome.

The tax code will always guide you to wealth. It is the blueprint. As of 2017, the Tax Cuts & Jobs Act increased the standard deduction and capped the amount of mortgage interest and property taxes an individual can take on their primary residence. Simultaneously, it also raised the standard deduction for each filing status. Essentially, if your mortgage interest and property taxes are not greater than your standard deduction, then you get absolutely no benefit. How many of you prepare your own taxes, plug in your mortgage interest and property taxes, and get the message, *"You are getting the standard deduction?"* That's because the tax code does not favor your primary residence. We are talking about wealth building. *If the tax code does not favor it, then it's not wealth building.*

The Tax Cuts & Jobs Act gave real estate investors bonus depreciation. This was normally not extended to regular investors like you and me. It was only reserved for new construction. As a result, we are now able to take advantage of huge phantom expenses that create phantom losses, as illustrated in our example, *and* use those phantom losses to offset all other income if we meet requirements to make the rental an active activity instead of a passive activity.

So, for people who feel falsely secure in having their own home, paying your carrying costs with that one stream of income—your W-2—I was there. I'm telling you, it's never going to work. And you will continue to be frustrated. You will continue to be paycheck to paycheck. You will continue to try to budget what hits your account. You will continuously be *stuck* in a corner.

CHAPTER 7

How to Maximize Your Tax Saving While Building Wealth

I've given you the tax codes that the average person, including myself, needs to build wealth. The tax code is thousands upon thousands of pages long. I have condensed the essential codes for you.
- Section 6001
- Section 162
- Section 179
- Section 469

So here we're actually going to move within the tax code. This is where you actually implement the strategies we talked about. Knowing them and actually executing them are two different things. Most people feel that operating within the tax code is a lot harder than it is. But it just seems more complex than it is. When the average person looks at the tax return, they get anxious because it looks like this big, complex form. But as you can see in previous chapters, I've actually broken it down with visual aids for you.

STEP ONE: CLEAR OUT BAD DEBT

Bad debt is debt incurred that doesn't produce cash flow or what I call tax flow (tax savings). Let's talk about where most people start. I want to stress this is not a "quit your 9–5" strategy. For the masses, for the most part, we must use our ordinary income—which is from our employment—to build extraordinary wealth. I am going to give an unpopular opinion, so brace for impact. I don't believe you can budget your way out of everything. Many people have crippling debt that prevents them from building wealth. Outside of having poor spending habits, if you are in a space where debt is killing your paycheck, get rid of it. No, it's not a magic wand that you wave around. Of course, I know you can't just *pay it off*... or can you? Let's take a walk down memory lane.

Remember in Chapter 1, I recounted paying off my student loans with my retirement funds. I then used my then-converted rental property to offset any taxes owed. The truth is, even if I couldn't utilize my rental property, I still would have taken the lump sum and paid off the loan. Why? Because it was a serious hindrance. I couldn't get approved for another loan. So that left me a sitting duck while I paid off the loan. Sound familiar?

So I did some number crunching—well... internet math. I Googled a loan amortization calculator. There are plenty at your fingertips. I wanted to see how *long* it would ultimately take me to pay off the loans and how much I would be paying in *interest* above the principal amount. Turns out it would take me 15 years to pay off the student loans and an additional $56,000 in interest, for a total of $141,000 (see below).

Loan Calculator

Amortized Loan: Paying Back a Fixed Amount Periodically
Use this calculator for basic calculations of common loan types such as mortgages, auto loans, student loans, or personal loans, or click the links for more detail.

Loan Amount	$85000
Loan Term	15 years
	0 months
Interest Rate	7.5 %
Compound	Monthly (APR)
Pay Back	Every Month

Results:
Payment Every Month $787.96
Total of 180 Payments $141,832.89
Total Interest $56,832.89
View Amortization Table

Then, I calculated separately what I would have in my retirement savings if I, in fact, didn't touch it for 15 years. Remember, as a wage earner with living expenses and student loan payments, I could only contribute so much. It turns out that I would lose out a total of $283,000. Again, I used a calculator online. No need for surgery when technology is at our fingertips.

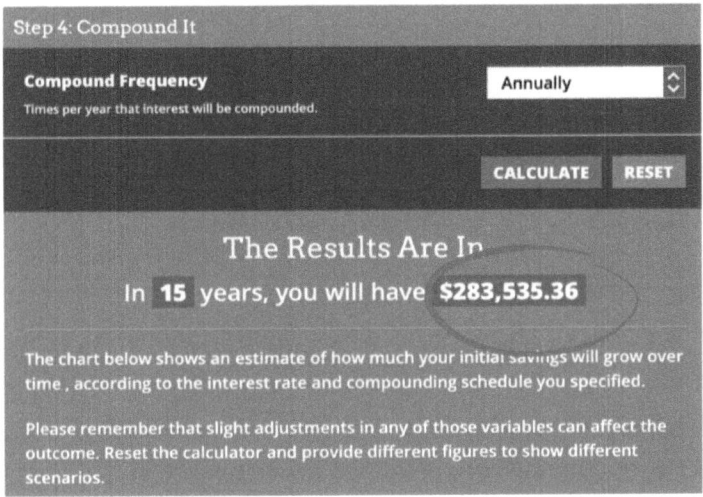

Is it perfect math? No. But it's good enough for me to do a cost-benefit analysis. What would it cost me to pay off the student loans with my retirement money? You may say $283,000. But I would also have paid out $141,000 in student loans, including the interest. *And* I would have lost 15 years living in a constant state of budgeting a paycheck or trying to make a larger salary. I was 35. I didn't want to be 50 trying to solidify my golden years.

Lastly, I did more internet math. What if I paid off the student loans with my retirement and was able to contribute the maximum amount for that same 15-year period to my retirement since the loans would be gone? Turns out, even starting at the age of 35 from close to scratch, I would have way more money without the student loan payments eating up my paycheck. $430,000 in 15 years with no student loans or tight contributions due to student loan payments and living expenses, with a balance of $283,000 *and* an additional $56,000 in interest paid out *and* 15 years of financial bondage.

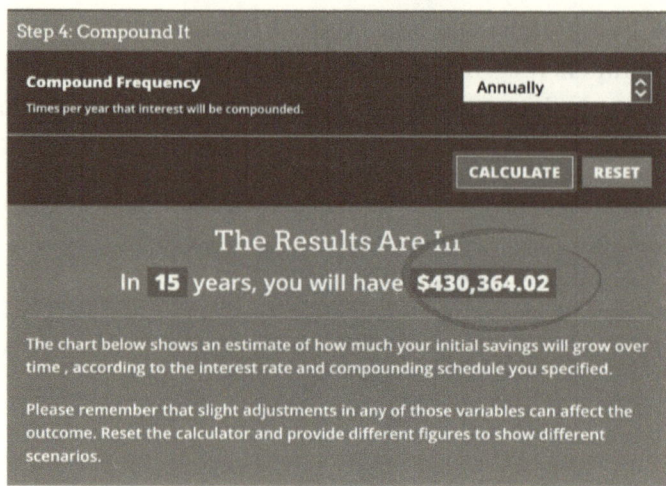

See where I'm going with this? These are *my* numbers. I encourage you to run your own numbers. I had to wipe out the debt that was holding me back. Debt that did not produce cash flow or tax savings. Debt that did not produce any wealth outside of retirement contributions. At 50 years of age, I would be closer to retirement than not. Many Americans cannot afford to retire comfortably, no matter how minimally they plan to live. You don't control the cost of eggs, milk or gas. You can't control your healthcare costs.

Removing the debt freed my income by over $700 a month. I had some cash flow from my rental and tax savings (tax flow) from my rental. I was clear to take off. No credit card debt and no student loans or personal loans. No auto loans.

If you find yourself unable to move with flexibility because of bad debt, I encourage you to run your own numbers. Again, even if I couldn't use my rental to offset taxes from the early withdrawal, I would still have done it to be free to operate outside of my wages from my employer.

Now, many will ask, "Why didn't you just take a loan from your retirement?" I was in the mindset of not being tied to my employer. If I left, I would owe, as the loan would become a distribution. If you're comfortable taking a loan from your retirement account instead, by all means, consider it. I wanted to cut all ties, and I don't regret my decision one bit.

I say this to encourage you to start utilizing your liquid resources. Budgeting works for short-term strategy. But as I stated earlier, there are some things you cannot budget your way out of. Holding on to what *could* be without acknowledging what *is* will leave you in the same cycle many are trapped in. I saved myself 15 years and tons of money. I now own several rental properties and have a great business, educating wage earners, business owners, and real estate investors on building wealth within the tax code. I couldn't have done this if I were still paying my expenses and student loans and contributing minimally to an employer-sponsored retirement plan. I never got attached to things. I was willing to sell my condo but couldn't. I was willing to empty my retirement out and did. I say this so you don't spend your best working years paying down debt that takes 10-plus years. Time is most important. Am I saying pull all your equity out of your home or sell it? Am I saying pull all money out of your retirement account? I'm saying run your own numbers to determine if you are holding on to a false dream while real numbers and time slip through your fingertips.

STEP TWO: DECIDE ON A ROUTE

We discussed the tax code hierarchy earlier in the book (see below).

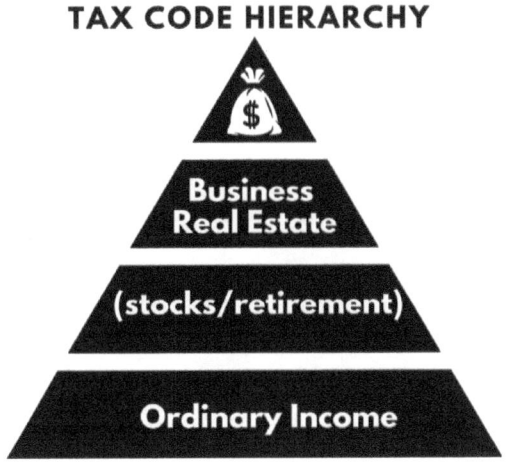

Make a decision on what is most attainable and how flexible you are. This looks different for everyone. So, I will give you a couple of scenarios to get you thinking.

You live in your primary residence with no rentals and earn a W-2 from your employer. Your first option would be to see what your numbers would look like if your primary residence were a rental or if you purchased a rental and how this would affect your taxes. Again, we utilize over-the-counter tax software in "Tax Strategies Mastermind" to track our tax liability and input scenarios. We don't commit to financial surgery with pen and paper. Simply input. Let the software run the numbers.

Perhaps you can't move out of your primary and convert it to a rental. Maybe you live close to family who help with childcare, or your kids are in an ideal school district and close to all their activities. Maybe the cost of moving and renting while you convert your primary is too high. Again, this is a cost analysis based on your situation. Singles may be able to move with more flexibility. Perhaps your significant other is okay with being flexible for a short period of time. All roads to growth are temporary upsets in your daily life. Your options are based on capability:

1. Real Estate

- Convert your primary residence to a rental.
- Purchase a rental property (make sure you have enough hours to make REPS or STR rules). Perhaps this may mean investing out of state. I'm from NYC, which is not a cash-flowing state for rentals. I had to look elsewhere. It required work. But I've had no tax liability as a result. I've saved over $500,000 in taxable income. Nothing is completely smooth, but it can be doable nevertheless.
- Connect and interview multiple real estate agents to choose someone knowledgeable in your rental market.
- Move to an area with several opportunities for investing, particularly in multifamily properties.
- If you go the real estate route, which strategy is best for you? If you are a full-time wage earner, or both spouses are full-time

wage earners, you have to consider short-term rentals. Are you willing to put in the work to make the hours requirements? What is your tax liability on your current paycheck? Would you like that back in your bank account?

- Does one spouse work full-time, and the other is retired or works part-time? They may be able to make the REPS for long-term rentals and avoid the constant activity in short-term rentals.

2. Business Ownership

You may be more inclined to start a business, as the financial barrier to entry may be significantly less than closing costs. Perhaps you already have a business that you are dabbling in. Starting a business can be relatively easy, depending on the type of business. It's only hard because there's no structure for the average person. They don't know where to start. That's where I come in.

- Decide on what your business will be. What product or service will you offer? What *value* will it provide to the end user, your customer? It must exceed the cost of your service. My Mastermind is set at $2,997 for a lifetime membership. The average tax refund is $2,500. The average tax savings from my students is upwards of $40,000 per year. See how the value outweighs the cost?
- If you don't know what business to start, that requires introspection. If you are knowledgeable on a topic, *master* it. Provide education on the topic. Someone is your audience.
- Start the activities checklist I've provided below. You don't have to do everything at once, but do one thing a day or three things per weekend.
- Choose a name.
- Check the U.S. Patent and Trademark Office website to see if your name is available.
- Check any social media handles to see if your name is available.

- If your name is available on all social media platforms and the U.S. Patent and Trademark Office, secure it. Have an attorney start the trademark process for you. Secure the social media handles immediately. That's free.
- Secure your business email. You can do this in a number of ways. Google's G Suite allows you to customize your business email, e.g. support@themoneynista.com rather than a Gmail extension.
- Secure a web hosting service. You will need a place to send your customers to learn about you. A website is important. It doesn't need to be super complex. Simple and easy to navigate is best. Squarespace is a great starter for new business owners. If you don't feel comfortable, you can outsource to a graphic designer. There are plenty on Fiverr.com, and you can even do an Instagram search.
- Decide if you are serious about your business, meaning you are ready to engage. If not, you can remain a sole proprietorship until you begin. If you are ready to start operations, form your LLC with your state's secretary of state website. This is immediate for most states. You will get the Articles of Organization immediately in email.
- You will need an Employer Identification Number (an EIN) for your business. This is free on the IRS website. Simply visit www.irs.gov and in the search bar and type *"EIN."* You will see the link immediately, then follow the prompts discussed earlier. The IRS site assigns an EIN immediately on Form SS-4. It's important to note that if you have more than one business, each should have its own EIN and business structure.
- Take your Articles of Organization (AOO) and Form SS-4 down to a trusted bank and open your business bank account. Make sure you have two forms of identification, like your license and passport or credit card. Some banks have different ID requirements, so it may be a good idea to call in advance.
- Inquire about a business credit card as well. If you have decent credit, this shouldn't be an issue. Remember, we cleared out all bad debt already.

- Next, link your business bank account to all forms of payment you accept. They could be a third-party payment processor like Stripe, Square, etc. Whatever works best for you, but whatever you do, make sure that it's linked *only* to your business bank account.
- Link your business credit card to all payment sources. If you run Facebook ads, link your business credit card to the Meta Business Suite. If you have an email service provider, link your business credit card to the billing. Essentially, anything that is ordinary and necessary for your business links to the credit card for the recurring expense. Then, pay your credit card from your business bank account.
- If you find yourself not having enough income in your bank account for expenses, do not pay your business expenses from your personal bank account. Simply transfer the funds to your business bank account, then pay the credit card. No business payments should come from your personal bank account.

It's important to keep all business activities separate not only from your personal activities but from other unrelated businesses if you have more than one business.

The reason for this is recordkeeping. Remember the golden rule: Recordkeeping is the most important tax code for any business activity. It's easy to download your monthly expenses from each business from your dedicated business credit card and your record of income from your dedicated business bank account. We use this method in "Tax Strategies Mastermind" when tracking our tax liability monthly.

The last items are for when you utilize strategies like hiring your children and/or eventually designating S-corp status and paying yourself a salary. You must hire a payroll company. Popular ones are Gusto Inc. and ADP Payroll Solutions. You set your account up online with your business information, including your name and EIN, and any employees, such as your kids, other family members, or even others you may hire. You can also link your independent contractors to your payroll company and manually run payroll when the contractor needs to be paid. This is best, as the payroll company keeps track of all contractors and prepares and sends the 1099s by the required date of January 31st of every year, and in most cases, will file the 1099s to the IRS for you. If you miss this deadline, you will incur penalties.

Starting tax year 2023, if you have ten or more information returns, such as 1099s, you must file them electronically. Again, this is best if you sign up with a payroll company. Even if you are a real estate investor and you have many contractors that work on your property per year, having them registered with your payroll company eliminates any missed deadlines.

If you want to prepare your 1099s manually—which I don't recommend—you can issue them to your contractors by the deadline of January 31 of every year and file them for free through the IRS taxpayer portal. Again, not recommended. For my business owners and real estate investors, I outsource it to a payroll company. They will do all the required filings. They will solicit the Form W-9 and collect the information needed from the contractor before you engage in any work. This way, you don't have to worry about taking a deduction for the amount you paid a contractor with no information to issue a 1099 to them. Remember, an expense to you is income to someone else.

If you, as the owner, are on payroll, you have assessed the ability to pay yourself a reasonable salary. See the previous chapter on the tax codes you need to know under Section 162 Owner's Compensation. This is when you set up your retirement plan, either a SEP IRA or Solo 401(k), depending on if you are an owner with employees other than your spouse. Revisit Chapter 3 for a refresher.

I've provided a list below for your convenience.

If you are already a business owner, chances are you're not putting enough money into your business. Most wage earners who are engaged in a business outside of their employer are budgeting business expenditures. By spending the money in your business, you are earning back the withholdings from your employer's pay. It's coming out of your paycheck anyway. Why not earn it back by spending on your business for your own growth? Even if you have a business loss, that loss will offset your withholdings. Simultaneously, you are expanding your business much more rapidly.

Business Activities Checklist

- [ ] Domain Name
- [ ] Trademark Name (Application)
- [ ] Instagram Name
- [ ] Facebook Name
- [ ] Twitter Name
- [ ] YouTube Channel Name
- [ ] Web Hosting Service (I.e Squarespace)
- [ ] Payment Processor (Through web hosting service?)
- [ ] Business Designation (S Corp/LLC)
- [ ] Credit Card Designation PER BUSINESS (EIN)
- [ ] Bank Account Designation PER business (EIN)

Business Activities Checklist

- [ ] Link All Expense Accounts to appropriate Credit Card (Web Hosting, Email Marketing subscription, FB/IG ads, etc.

- [ ] Link All Payment Processors to Accounts appropriate Bank Account (Venmo/Stripe/ Sam Cart, etc)

- [ ] Payroll Company Set Up (I.e Gusto)

- [ ] Retirement Plan Setup (SEP/Solo 401K)

- [ ] Software Purchase (TuborTax Business/Home & Business

So we've cleared our bad debt, decided on real estate and/or business ownership, and started our paperwork and foundation for activities. Now we have to engage in the actual deductions outside of start-up costs and activities. Your everyday activities should be deductible for the most part outside of your employer.

HIGH-IMPACT STRATEGIES FIRST

Within the hierarchy of the tax code, there's a hierarchy of deductions you should aim for. Again, there's a formula. Then, there's a formula within the formula. Engage in real estate and/or business ownership first. Then, within that strategy, attack the high-impact deductions.

1. Your Vehicle

As discussed earlier, if you use your vehicle for over 50% of the time for business, you can take the Section 179 deduction, provided your vehicle meets the weight requirements discussed. You will also be eligible for bonus depreciation within the Tax Cuts & Jobs Act rules. You must document the use of your vehicle. If you use it to go to properties during repairs and maintenance, document the miles. MileIQ is a good app. If you visit clients in your business, document each trip and the purpose of each trip. This is a great high-impact deduction for business owners. Remember, bonus depreciation is only in the first year you place the asset in service, and it has an expiration date in the Tax Cuts & Jobs Act.

2. Rental Property

If you are going the investor route, again, bonus depreciation is a huge tax savings event. You can create huge losses without spending an actual dime and then offset all other income with a Real estate professional status or short-term rental strategy. Again, though, remember that bonus depreciation has an expiration date.

3. Tools/Machinery/Equipment

For my business owners, bonus depreciation is also applicable within the Tax Cuts & Jobs Act. Have a tow truck company? Tractor-trailer? Printing Press? All of these are items that can utilize what we call "expense acceleration" (bonus depreciation) in the first year.

4. Retirement

As a business owner, you can open up a SEP IRA or Solo 401(k) (please see the previous chapter for differences) and contribute up to 25% of your compensation from your business, not to exceed limits for the attributable year. The limits are often three times greater than regular employee contributions. For 2024, the limit is $69,000. So if you are doing well in your business in 2024 and are able to compensate yourself as the owner (S-corp) up to $280,000, you can contribute the max to a retirement plan. This amount is also deducted from your business income, which lowers your taxable income.

5. Hiring Kids

Who else should you pay a salary to work in your business but the kiddos? Pay them up to the standard deduction for single filers, and they will have no tax liability. You, as the employer, can deduct this expense from your business income. You can also contribute to an employer-sponsored retirement plan for your kids who are employed by your business. This is also expensed in your business. They must be on salary and not 1099, or they will be subject to self-employment taxes. This means they are on payroll.

6. Expense Acceleration

We talked about bonus depreciation and Section 179. These are both a form of expense acceleration, which means you get to take the majority of the expense in one year. For these, it's the first year the asset is in service. However, there are other expense acceleration techniques. If you find yourself owing taxes during the year, you can increase your advertising costs or even increase your salary. You can buy the equipment you need for your business. Maybe you are a real estate investor and have been meaning to replace that cracked bathroom vanity in one of your rental properties. For this to work, you will need to track your tax liability in real time. In "Tax Strategies Mastermind," we keep track of our monthly income and expenses (recordkeeping) and utilize over-the-counter software to plan for the current year. If we, as planners, see that current numbers at any point in the year will yield us a tax liability, we utilize expense acceleration techniques. This doesn't work if you aren't tracking your tax liability in real time.

7. Leftover Deductions

I call these leftover because the average small business owner doesn't realize these don't have the best impact and often have high audit adjustments.

Augusta Rule: The Augusta Rule, known to the IRS as Section 280A, allows homeowners to rent out their home for up to 14 days per year without needing to report the rental income on their individual tax return. What most people attempt to do is to force as much income in those 14 days so that it's not taxable. The IRS still holds the "ordinary and necessary" rule here. If your business rents your personal residence for up to 14 days for the year, and you are audited, the income will show on the bank statement for the business, and an examiner will likely ask for all personal bank statements for all savings and checking accounts. If you are a business owner and you decide to rent your home out to your business for, say, meetings or networking events, make sure the rental rate is market rate for your area and duration of time. Always think about audits over income when building your wealth through the U.S. Tax Code.

Home Office: This is a popular one, but to be honest, it doesn't move mountains. There's rarely any movement in tax liability with the home office deduction. I call it a "feel good" deduction because it makes you feel good, but you don't really save thousands, if even hundreds of dollars. If you are entitled to it, take it. But it shouldn't be your strategy; it should be more like an afterthought.

Medical Expenses: This is the only time I will mention a deduction on Form 1040. Your medical expenses would have to exceed 7.5% of your adjusted gross income for a benefit to be realized. Let's say your adjusted gross income is $80,000 to make this simple. You can only expense medical and dental costs that exceed $6,000. So, if you had a medical bill that wasn't covered by insurance totaling $10,000, you can deduct $4,000. Of course, as your salary increases, it becomes difficult to benefit.

The goal is to maximize and reach for breadcrumbs in the tax code. Low-hanging fruit usually isn't worth it. This is why millions of dollars are lost to the tax liabilities of individuals. They don't know their options. I can't tell you how many times I've heard, "My preparer never told me this," or "Can you direct me to a CPA?" Preparers are just that. They prepare taxes. You sought out a tax preparer and really want tax advisory services. You also assume a CPA (certified public accountant) is a tax professional. Accountancy is a large umbrella. You have CPAs that are auditors, preparers, comptrollers, etc., but they don't have tax knowledge. There are CPAs that specialize in tax. My point is, don't assume the title means knowledge. Much like your general physician, they must refer you to specialists. One doctor doesn't take care of all ailments and health issues. You have different doctors that specialize.

CHAPTER 8

The Ideal Marriage

RECAP OF KEY POINTS

By now, you understand real wealth is in business activities, including real estate. The ideal is to marry the two so that you reap the benefits. Many of you are experts at a subject that is very necessary or caters to an audience. As of January 2024, there are 344 million people in the United States alone and 8 billion people in the world. Someone is your customer, your client, your tenant, or your student. Start from the top of the tax code hierarchy and work your way down.

- Clear out all consumer (bad) debt. This is any debt that doesn't produce cash flow or tax flow (tax savings).
- Start allocating your ordinary income to business or real estate activities. Never leave ordinary income on the table (talk to the tax code). Spend the money. Uncle Sam is taking it out of your check anyway, so you may as well earn it back during filing season.
- Form your business structure after you are out of the start-up phase, including obtaining your Employer Identification Number (EIN).
- Open a business bank account under your EIN and obtain a business credit card as well. Make sure *only* business income and expenses are allocated to each respectively.

- Keep clean books and records, as this is the most important part of your foundation. When in doubt, over-document.
- For real estate investors: Decide on a long-term rental strategy (REPS) or the short-term rental (STR) loophole, depending on your employment situation. Visit REPStracker.com and create an account to start logging your hours for each strategy (promo code: "Moneynista"). Be sure to upload any and all documentation with each activity you log (invoices, estimates, emails, contracts, screenshots, etc.).
- Try to do both.

Items of Consideration

As of now, Congress has considered the extension of 100% bonus depreciation. Instead of the current schedule, as discussed in the real estate and business ownership strategies, this is a big deal as it creates a huge phantom loss due to huge phantom expenses that offset real income. As of now, 100% bonus depreciation is only extended to qualified property placed in service (ready and available for use) between September 27, 2017, and December 31, 2022. The amount begins to phase out in 2023 to 80%, then 60% in 2024, 40% in 2025, and finally 20% in 2026. It will be completely phased out to 0% in 2027.

Congress has partially voted on the extension of 100% bonus depreciation. The bill would retroactively allow taxpayers to claim 100% bonus depreciation for property placed in service between January 1, 2023, and December 31, 2025. Property placed in service after December 31, 2025, and before January 1, 2027, would be allowed 20% bonus depreciation. For property placed in service after January 1, 2027, no bonus depreciation would be allowed.

Trust and Estate Planning

Building wealth through the tax code, which is the only way to build wealth in the United States, requires long-term planning: time, energy, and money. You may not have a lot now, but beginning your journey through this newfound information, you will want to protect it. The first thing you're thinking about is creditors or lawsuits. I'm thinking beyond that, taking family into consideration as well. It's not enough to have a living will. You must consider a trust. A trust is a tool to shelter taxes to your heirs as well as to give instructions on how you want your assets managed in your passing. Most wealth is lost due to death and subsequent mismanagement of assets by those who are left behind. Nothing is as detrimental to wealth as a fight after a funeral, such as arguing over who gets the grandparents' or parents' home. Even if it's just the family home, it's an asset if it's paid off. Leaving it to the living without instruction is dangerous.

Imagine working and paying off a 30-year mortgage for it all to go down the drain due to a lack of property tax payments or fighting amongst siblings during probate. What a waste! The "generation" of generational wealth has to be managed, even beyond the grave. Don't forget about your retirement accounts. You must designate beneficiaries. Leave no stone unturned. Talk to your local trust and estate planning attorney. Whether it's a simple Google search or by referral of a friend, colleague, or neighbor, give them all the details of your assets, who you want them left to, and any special instructions, and let them set up the appropriate structure for you. It will cost you, but it will be one of the best investments you make. If you have no beneficiaries or heirs, consider a charity. Just don't let it go back to the state!

Case Study

Yours truly started as a wage earner. It took me five jobs and 19 years to understand and implement. I want to save you the time and headache of trial and error. My business started as a Schedule C. I didn't know how my services would be received. I needed to know there was a place for my knowledge, and what better way than social media? I mainly used Instagram, and I have to tell you, I wasn't social media savvy. Once I started to build up my following, I dedicated one personal credit card for all ads/boosts of my posts to gain awareness. I allocated some of my paychecks every pay period to both save for my multifamily and pump into Moneynista. I used that time to build out "Tax Strategies Mastermind" using Canva, a graphic design app. I also purchased my first multifamily property in the interim with my savings and employer wages.

By the time I was ready to release Mastermind, showing I was dedicated and ready to go and had an audience, I decided to form my LLC. I had done a pre-sale and knew I was ready to go. Right away, I did the reasonable salary test and designated S-corp so I could pay myself a salary. In the interim, I had to leave my job so I could pursue my business full-time. Was I scared? I don't remember. I felt like the transition was seamless. I had no bad debt outstanding and a decent retirement account by that time, as I had seven years of maximum contributions to my employer plan after clearing most of it out in 2014 for my student loans. I had a plan. I wasn't afraid to fail, but I was afraid to not try. Don't tell yourself you don't have the money. Just reposition your funds. In fact, if you are reading this book, you definitely have some wiggle room. It doesn't have to be overnight. It took me about 1.5 years. You would be surprised how quickly things turn around.

I eventually rolled over my employer retirement funds to my SEP IRA because now I was a business owner. I even continued to use retirement funds to purchase real estate. I had no tax liability because I used bonus depreciation and REPS. The tax code does not recognize income offset by phantom losses. I had no tax liability and paid no taxes on my salary. The losses offset my wages from my business and my business profits. That is what I want for you. I didn't *wake* up a millionaire. I *worked* up to being a millionaire. I started at 35 by making a scary decision, pulling funds from my retirement. I earned 15 years of my life and out-earned any perceived losses I would have taken. I didn't have a rich dad or poor dad, a rich mom or poor mom. Just working-class parents. I learned to save and budget from them. I didn't learn to build wealth until I started to absorb the tax code through my career.

Example: Here is an example of how to pay no taxes while building wealth. Consider the following facts:

S-corp K-1 (income - expenses)	$300,000
Salary To Owner from S-corp	$280,000
Total amounts reported on Form 1040	$580,000

Real Estate Losses	($650,000)
Taxable Income	($70,000)

Do you see how that works? All profits and salaries from the S-corp are not taxable because real estate losses offset all the income due to REPS. Additionally, there's a $70,000 loss to carry forward to the next year to offset income in this example.

If there is no real estate or you've exhausted all your current real estate losses, you, as a business, can manage your tax liability by increasing expenses in real time. It's called expense acceleration. Remember to contribute to your retirement plan, whether it's a Solo 401(k) or a SEP IRA. Pay yourself a reasonable salary, pay your kids a reasonable salary, and put the money into operating expenses, like advertising and professional consultations like estate and tax planning. Remember, as a business, you can determine where to spend the money before it becomes taxable.

Conclusion

As a tax strategist with thousands of students, we have saved well over $10 Million in taxable income and counting in the last three years. Money Masters Academy's "Tax Strategies Mastermind" is a hands-on approach in which I guide you using visual tools year after year to build wealth. To enroll, visit www.themoneynista.com and hit the "Enroll" button. The cost is a one-time fee for lifetime access, including any tax law updates. You will also be admitted to the private Facebook group and have dedicated email access to a tax professional on demand. The course allows you to go at your own pace and is guaranteed to turn your life around when you apply these strategies, especially with an expert coach on hand.

I was able to go from paycheck to paycheck to multi-millionaire by moving within the U.S. tax code. You can, too! Take a look at the curriculum below and I hope to see you there!

Money Masters Academy "Tax Strategies Mastermind" Curriculum

Orientation
Business Activities
    Business Activities Defined
    Formation
    Trademark
    Trademark Search Tool Tutorial
    Books & Records (IRC Section 6001)
    Building your Books & Records

- Business Credit
  - Understanding Financials and Building Business Credit
- Business Structure
  - Intro
  - Sole Proprietorship/Single-Member LLC
  - Multi-Member LLC/Partnership
  - S Corporation
  - C Corporation
  - Tax Withholding Estimator Tutorial-Quarterly Taxes
- Business Deductions (IRC Section 162)
  - Key Terms & Definitions
  - Tax Reductions
  - Officers Compensation
  - Determining Reasonable Compensation
  - Salaries & Wages
  - Salaries & Wages Strategy
  - Understanding Child Labor Laws
  - Hiring Yourself & Others (Gusto)
  - Repairs & Maintenance
  - Bad Debts/Rents/Advertising
  - Travel, Meals & Entertainment
  - Section 179 Vehicle Deduction
  - Business Vehicle Input for Sole Proprietorship/Single-Member LLC
  - Business Vehicle Input for S Corporation/ Multi-Member LLC
  - Other Deductions
  - PDF Attachment: Tax Deductions Checklist For Business Owners
- Tax Avoidance: Real Estate
  - Intro
  - Depreciation
  - Cost Segregation (Bonus Depreciation) Free Benefit Estimate
- Real Estate Professional Status
  - Documentation: REPStracker
  - REPStracker Tutorial
  - Lease Protection Insurance
- Next Steps

Capital Gains
Real Estate Strategy
Long-Term Rental Strategy (REPS)- Sole Proprietors/Single-Member LLC
    Entering Rental Property
    Bonus Depreciation- Long-Term Rentals
    Carry Forward Losses- Long-Term Rentals
Short-Term Rental Strategy- Sole Proprietors/Single-Member LLC
    Bonus Depreciation- Short-Term Rentals
    Long-Term Rental Strategy (REPS)- Multi-Member LLC
    Short-Term Rental Strategy- Multi-Member LLC

Tax Deferral
    Retirement Planning

Planning and Preparation
    Intro
    Sole Proprietorship/Single-Member LLC Return Input and Planning
    Multi-Member LLC Return Input and Planning
    S-corp Return Input and Planning
    Monthly Live Q&As, including dedicated student email access and private Facebook group.

THANK YOU FOR READING MY BOOK!

Just to say thanks for buying and reading my book, I would like to give you access to a bonus training, no strings attached!

Scan the QR code:

I appreciate your interest in my book and value your feedback as it helps me improve future versions of this book. I would appreciate it if you could leave your invaluable review on Amazon.com with your feedback. Thank you!

www.ingramcontent.com/pod-product-compliance
Lightning Source LLC
Chambersburg PA
CBHW030247010526
44107CB00031B/1351/J